This book is dedicated to the memory of Samantha Runnion.
Samantha was a beautiful, bright, and joyful little girl and a
precious gift to all who knew her.

Samantha Runnion
July 26, 1996–July 15, 2002

Endorsements

"The radKIDS Personal Empowerment Safety and Life Skills Educational Organization is honored to recognize the incredible work of Mary in this book and her efforts to bring forth a conversation and a call to action on protecting our children from the ever increasing pandemic of pornography and the violence and victimization associated with the proliferation of pornography in our world today. Thanks to our ever increasing technology and access to information our children are exposed to much more unsolicited and unsupervised information then any generation before them. This exposure to information without proper context and educated and supervised communication continues to expand exponentially each day. Mary's effort to share this exposure and the effects on our children's life is commendable, and even though it may be hard to read, the time has long come for the discussion. Education is the only thing that can truly change fear into power and Mary's efforts in *The Guardians of Innocence* is a great step in that direction."

—STEPHEN M. DALEY, *MEd, executive director and founder of the radKIDS Personal Empowerment Safety Education Program, www.radKIDS.org*

"I am most pleased and honored to see this book published. *The Guardians of Innocence* has the powerful capability of doing so much good. I professionally work with parents and children and know the challenge of the struggles with this addiction. *The Guardians* will be extremely helpful in encouraging communication between parents and children, and it will help both of them come to an understanding of the ways and means to cope with the challenges of the terrible nature of pornography's addictive process."

—DR. W. DEAN BELNAP, *Specialist in Pediatrics and Child/Adolescent Psychiatry.*

"We now live in a culture in which sexual gratification has become of greater importance in relationships than any other consideration. Our mass media have transformed the image of the ideal woman from being a compassionate into a dispassionate sex object. History confirms that any society whose culture is so totally focused on self-gratification will soon disappear. Mary Muller has provided an inspired warning to all who have any concern regarding our ultimate destiny. This book is worthy of your serious study. The author is worthy of your sincere gratitude."

—JOHN HARMER, *former Lt. Governor and senator of California;*
Chairman of the Lighted Candle Society

"I deeply appreciate Mary Muller's courage, passion, compassion and conviction in a great effort to educate and inspire others to pick up the banner and fight against the insidious traumas that can be caused by pornography. Why do pornographers make pornography? Because they value money over human lives, commitments, and respect. As a psychologist who has treated pornography addiction for almost two decades, I echo Mary's thoughts—pornography can be one of the most damaging and addictive influences ever encountered. I encourage anyone and everyone to read these pages and become informed about the new tobacco of our age. Thank you, Mary!"

—DR. RANDALL HYDE, *Licensed Clinical Psychologist,*
Owner/Clinical Director of Private Mental Health Clinic,
Chief Psychologist/ Director for Regional Mental Health Hospital

"I am in complete *awe* of what Mary has accomplished with her book! This is the most complete, comprehensive work on the subject of protecting children from the dangers of pornography that I have ever read. Pornography is now at the forefront of addictive behaviors that threaten not only the minds and souls of our children, but society at large. I strongly encourage you to take the information in this remarkable book to heart and educate yourselves—as the author says—if for no other reason than for the sake of the children. Mary's book is a must read for parents and for all adults."

—MARK B. KASTLEMAN, *Cofounder of candeocan.com;*
author and international trainer for pornography
addiction prevention and healing

The
Guardians of
INNOCENCE

The Guardians of INNOCENCE

A Parent's Guide to Protecting Children from Pornography

MARY MULLER

Horizon Books
Springville, Utah

ISBN 13: 978-0-88290-979-0

Published by Horizon Books, an imprint of Cedar Fort, Inc., 2373 W. 700 S., Springville, UT 84663
Distributed by Cedar Fort, Inc., www.cedarfort.com

LIBRARY OF CONGRESS CATALOGING-IN-PUBLICATION DATA

Library of Congress Cataloging-in-Publication Data

Muller, Mary Margaret, author.
  The guardians of innocence : a parent's guide to protecting children from pornography / Mary Margaret Muller.
    p. cm.
  Summary: Educates parents and guardians on the many ways to protect and prevent their children from viewing and/or becoming addicted to pornography.
  ISBN 978-0-88290-979-0
  1. Children and pornography. 2. Internet and children. 3. Internet pornography. 4. Children--Crimes against--Prevention. 5. Internet--Security measures. I. Title.

  HQ784.S45.M85 2011
  649'.7--dc22

2011001587

Cover design by Megan Whittier
Cover design © 2011 by Lyle Mortimer
Edited and typeset by Melissa J. Caldwell

Printed in the United States of America

10 9 8 7 6 5 4 3 2 1

Printed on acid-free paper

CONTENTS

ACKNOWLEDGMENTS

I am particularly grateful for the shared knowledge and cooperation of the following individuals that so willingly supported my efforts to research and write *The Guardians of Innocence*. Thank you for allowing me to quote your materials and glean from your years of hard work fighting to protect society from the disastrous effects of pornography.

Dr. W. Dean Belnap—is a specialist in pediatric and child/adolescent psychiatry, Fellow of the American Academy of Pediatrics, the American Psychiatric Association, the Society of Behavioral Pediatrics, the American Society of Adolescent Psychiatry, and the American Neuropsychiatric Association. He's been the director of nationwide psychiatric hospitals, and elected or appointed to more boards, councils, and associations than we can list here. He's a prolific writer, author (including *A Brain Gone Wrong*), and dedicated humanitarian.

John Harmer—has forty years of experience as an attorney and an elected public official (former Lt. Governor and senator of California). He has collaborated on many legal briefs presented to various courts on pornography cases, including the Supreme Court of the United States. He is an author of various publications (including *The Sex Industrial Complex*) and is the current Chairman of the Lighted Candle Society.

Dr. Donald L. Hilton Jr.—specialist in neurological surgery and named repeatedly to Best Doctors in America. He has published medical book chapters and journal articles and lectures nationally and internationally. He is also currently a clinical associate professor of neurosurgery at the University of Texas Medical School. Author of *He Restoreth My Soul*, he and his wife are program coordinators in San Antonio, Texas, for those who struggle with pornography and sexual addiction and for their spouses.

Dr. Randall F. Hyde, Dr. Bernell L. Christensen, and Mark B. Kastleman—cofounders of Candeo, LLC, and cocreators of Candeo's online pornography addiction psycho-education and recovery training program. All prolific speakers, authors, and trainers; Dr. Hyde is a licensed clinical psychologist, Dr. Christensen is a licensed marriage and family therapist, and Mark Kastleman is the author of *The Drug of the New Millennium*. All have helped thousands of individuals, couples, and families internationally in many areas including pornography/sexual addictions.

Shelley Lubben—"ex–porn star loving people out of porn," American missionary, executive director, the Pink Cross Foundation.

Dr. Jill Manning—marriage and family therapist, specializes in research and clinical work related to pornography and problematic sexual behavior. Lecturer, author (including *What's the Big Deal about Pornography*), researcher, and the source of testimony before governmental committees.

Robert Peters, Esq.—attorney, lecturer, author. He has drafted state and local obscenity and related laws and testified before state, local, and US senate legislative bodies. He has also authored amicus curiae briefs for the Court of Appeals, the D.C. circuit, and the US Supreme Court in support of federal laws regulating indecent material by means of broadcast and cable TV, telephone ("dial-a-porn") services, and computer. He is General Counsel and President Emeritus of Morality in Media.

Dr. Judith Reisman—veteran pornography researcher, author, and expert witness before the Attorney General's Commission on pornography. She specializes in the communication effects of images on the brain, mind, and memory; fraud in the human sexuality field; and the addictive properties of sexually explicit images. She has lectured and testified the world over to professional organizations, legislatures, parliaments, and courts. She has served as a consultant to the US Departments of Justice, Education, and Health and Human Services and has held academic positions at George Mason University, the American University, and the University of Haifa, Israel.

Erin D. Runnion—mother of Samantha Runnion and founding director of the Joyful Child Foundation, which is dedicated to preventing child sexual abuse and abduction. She has created programs that unite and uplift our nation's communities in the protection and wonderment of all children. She is also on the policy advisory board of the National Association to Protect Children and serves as a member of the Surviving Parents Coalition.

Ralph Yarro—former Novell executive; now a self-funded computer entrepreneur. Yarro's nonprofit organization, CP80 Foundation, www.cp80.org, gives us cyberspace tools to fight this battle. A Utah-based nonprofit organization dedicated to creating a more responsible and manageable Internet.

Dr. Kimberly Young—psychologist and internationally known expert on Internet addiction and online behavior. She has been invited to lecture at dozens of universities and conferences including the European Union of Health and Medicine in Norway and the First International Congress on Internet Addiction in Zurich. Director of the Center for Internet Addiction Recovery, expert witness, researcher, author, (including *Caught in the Net*). Professor at St. Bonaventure University, she serves on the editorial board of CyberPsychology and Behavior and the International Journal of Cyber Crime and Criminal Justice. She is a member of more boards and the recipient of more awards than can be mentioned herein.

A special thanks to Lyle Mortimer and Jennifer Fielding, at Cedar Fort, Inc. for their patience and dedication to this book, and to my friend Norma Murray, English instructor and invaluable proofreader.

My gratitude also to the many other individuals and organizations who allowed me to quote them herein. I am grateful to all unmentioned individuals who work to protect our children.

INTRODUCTION

Propaganda must be addressed to the emotions and not to the intelligence . . . vicious and gruesome, with lurid photographs. . . . Sexual and physical . . . the masses need . . . a thrill of horror.

ADOLF HITLER

This book will at times lower you into the mind-altering, dark, and ugly world of the sex industry. To cement the message of the entire book, there was absolutely no way around that.

Some children will view, or actually are viewing, the vilest and most horrific pornography. Parents and caregivers—all adults—need to know exactly what images are being dangerously imprinted into the minds of our youth and the resulting consequences.

Countless websites contain sexual and violent images that are available and free not only for adults, but for children of all ages to view. There's also cable TV, videos, Internet access on cell phones, gaming, and "pay-per-view" Internet sites (paid for with credit cards) that provide soft- and hard-core porn. Both the free (which can also be downloaded from the Internet onto mobile devices) and the pay-per-view sites provide everything from soft-core porn (erotic content with unsafe sex galore) to hard-core pornography.

1

Hard-core pornography involves sex with animals, children, corpses, and adolescents, and it may involve violence, bondage, group sex, prostitution, rape, and sodomy involving weapons (such as knives or broken glass, inanimate objects, and so on) used to sodomize the victim. Also included would be sexual activities involving defecation, urination, and vomit. And last, but not least, it can include hard-core torture, mutilation, and snuff films.

Any decent person can't possibly perceive the viewing of graphic, vile, and violent sex as acceptable entertainment for children. Common sense should tell us that when children are exposed to these graphic depictions, their attitudes about sexual behavior and humanity itself can have lifelong negative consequences.

If you have the Internet in your home, you have pornography in your home—seen or unseen (and just one mouse click away). "Nearly seven in ten (69%) teens ages 12–17 have a computer."[1] That large percentage doesn't even include those who view a friend's or relative's computer or computers at local schools and libraries.

> Nine out of ten children between eight and sixteen with Internet access have viewed pornography on the Internet. In most cases, the sex sites were accessed unintentionally when a child, often in the process of doing homework, used a seemingly innocent-sounding word to search for information or pictures.[2]

Also, if your youth has a mobile device with Internet access or photo capability they have access to pornography: "93% of teens ages 12–17 go online, as do 93% of young adults ages 18–29."[3] And obviously, mobile devices, along with gaming boxes, are what push the percentages of Internet access to pornography to even higher levels.

> The Internet is a powerful resource through which youth can access information, entertainment, and social connection. While it is important to ensure our youth have access to this increasingly important medium, it is equally important to minimize the

associated risks of sexual solicitation, abuse, harassment, and exposure to obscenity in the virtual square.

The number of children exposed to such risks is unfortunately increasing as Internet usage starts earlier and becomes more popular.

For example, "between 1998 and 2001, Internet usage among 3- to 4-year-olds jumped from 4.1 percent to 14.3 percent; 5- to 9-year-olds experienced a 16.8 percent to 38.9 percent increase; and 14- to 17-year-olds experienced a 51.2 percent to 75.6 percent hike in Internet usage."[4]

There's another aspect of pornography viewing that should strike a sickening fear into the heart of all decent people—the Internet is used by pedophiles (those who are sexually aroused by children). Some pedophiles (who can easily progress into child predators) may even already know your child; they could be someone as close to your child as their own parent or sibling. Pedophiles commonly use the Internet or porn videos to desensitize and "groom" children and teenagers, and it can be happening in your own living room or a trusted friend's home.

Child predators who are "strangers" to your child, usually act as "posers," befriending (grooming) your child online through the use of social networking, gaming sites, and Internet chat rooms to lure children into their clutches.

"Internet chat rooms resemble CB [citizens' band] channels in that they offer varying numbers of people the opportunity to listen and discuss specific topics. The number of CB radio channels is veritably small and is limited to available broadcast frequencies. At any one time on the Internet, however, there are typically about ten to twenty thousand 'channels' available to join."[5] Chat rooms are the playground of the pedophile.

Pedophiles use child pornography as a source for their own twisted entertainment, to view the most unthinkable violation of the innocent. Those images are routinely passed around and sadistically shared and discussed by the pedophiles. A huge number of the pornography sites on the Internet are those associated with child pornography.

For this reason alone, you need to read this book to acquaint yourself with the unthinkable—those addicted and sick predators whose lives revolve around the viewing of child pornography, their appetites fueled by the deviant acts they view and who can no longer satisfy their lust by inanimate images alone. They feed the ultimate cravings of their addiction by preying on the innocent and sometimes take their precious lives in the process.

After coming to a more horrific knowledge of the dangers of pornography to children, I came to the realization that in order to fully educate you, the reader, I would not be able to avoid Hitler's hypothesis of educating the masses with "horror."

The Guardians of Innocence, however, is not "propaganda" directed to the right hemisphere of your brain, as Hitler so utilized. It is comprised of legitimate and educated data and research from those who have worked with or studied and researched the topic for countless years. We now have irrefutable evidence through fMRIs of the actual brain damage. "This Neuroimagery is capable of observing and mapping the brain while the whole nervous system is carrying out its functions. These are not just fixed pictures of brain anatomy, but living, moving images."[6]

There's going to be a variety of readers, with a variety of viewpoints, who will, I hope, read this. Maybe you have a compulsive porn viewing tendency and you don't think you're hurting anyone. If you're simply a "recreational" soft-porn viewer who dances around the fringe of a dark abyss and thinks it's normal and harmless to go online occasionally for a sexual high, and you think you don't need to read this—then read it for the sake of the children.

Perhaps you're literally a closet porn addict yourself and you don't want this book in your home for fear that your spouse may read it and observe in you the warning signs. If that's the case, then unselfishly read it for the sake of the children whose developing brains can be permanently imprinted, rewired, and damaged for life with unimaginable images. Or read it for the safety of the children who will lose their precious innocence to other children who are acting out the deviancy they have seen in cyberspace or have been the victim of such perpetration themselves.

Perhaps you might feel that you don't need to read descriptive information on the evils of pornography because your children would never view such filth—that it would never happen to your child—then you really need to be warned. You need to know what your kids can be (or are being) exposed to and how to prevent, recognize, and deal with it.

Even on the off chance that your child would never view pornography of his own volition and doesn't have Internet access in your home, you need to read this because there's probably a preteen or a teen in your neighborhood right now that's seen sexual images you can't even imagine—a kid who might share their shocking entertainment with yours. It may even be from a group of kids your teen hangs out with, or your child's best friend, or a babysitter, or her boyfriend, or the older siblings of your child's friend, or someone's father, aunt, or uncle who's a porn addict or who might actually be sexually aroused by children (a pedophile).

Tragically, it might even be a sibling or parent that is preying upon him—a predator that sometimes can be the most intimidating and threatening for a child. It may be too difficult to comprehend, but incest happens more frequently than you can even begin to imagine in the seemingly best of families. The message here is not to start going on witch hunts—most adults who love and enjoy children are not pedophiles—so if you have suspicions of this kind of abuse (and showing pornography to a minor is also sexual abuse), don't let yourself jump to conclusions, but do not ignore an abused child. If you knowingly let this happen to any child and you do nothing about it, are you not also guilty of the damage that is being perpetrated upon the innocent?

Porn addicts come from all walks of life: they're judges, lawyers, doctors, law enforcers, religious leaders, scout leaders, teachers, baseball coaches, and the list goes on.

In addition, you will find that child advocates who are the guardians of children also come from all walks of life. I am a lay person (who relied on the combined knowledge of incredible experts) writing to a lay audience. However, I am only one of a myriad of dedicated individuals (the Erin Runnions, the John Walshes, the Ed Smarts, the Shelley Lubbens, and so many more) whose hearts were broken by the exploitation and victimization of children and who rechanneled their grief and anger into productive dedication toward child advocacy.

Exposure to pornography inflicts untold damage to the innocent. The entire issue of protecting children from this type of deviant tragedy and addiction while enabling them to take advantage of what can be the marvelous world of cyberspace is now one of the most critical challenges facing today's parents.

While the majority of information presented in this book emphasizes prevention, the treatment and healing of porn addiction is just as vital a concern.

Admittedly, *The Guardians of Innocence* does emphasize education on how to prevent the damage and addiction that the viewing of pornography can bring with it. Perhaps it may seem that I have somewhat ignored those who have already started down that path that for many sets in motion a life fraught with emotional destruction for them and people close to them. As put so well by Dr. Donald L. Hilton Jr.:

> We must also recognize that virtually all of our young men and many of our young women are already seriously exposed, and are therefore already in need of treatment. By continuing to emphasize avoidance only, we shame the majority who are already caught in the addition into secrecy and guilt. We must extend a hand of healing and support to those trapped in secrecy, so there is a safe place for them to seek help.[7]

Please know it is not my intention to shame or discourage anyone—only to educate all.

The data presented herein, with its sometimes disgusting descriptions of all the various twisted facets of pornography, cannot be explained without, perhaps, creating vivid and vile images in your mind's eye. I have no apologies for that because the children come first. Educate yourselves. Read this—if for no other reason than for the sake of the children.

—The Author

NOTES

1. See Amanda Lenhart, Kristen Purcell, Aaron Smith, and Kathryn Zickuhr, "Social Media & Mobile Internet Use among Teens and Young Adults," Pew Internet and American Life Project, 2007, accessed March 2010, http://www.pewinternet.org.

2. Mark B. Kastleman, *The Drug of the New Millennium—The Brain Science Behind Internet Pornography Use* (PowerThink Publishing, 2007), 6.

3. Lenhart, "Social Media & Mobile Internet," http://www.pewinternet.org.

4. Dr. Jill C. Manning, Testimony, *Hearing on Pornography's Impact on Marriage & the Family*, Subcommittee on the Constitution, Civil Rights, and Property Rights, Committee on Judiciary, United States Senate. November 10, 2005.

5. Patrick Carnes, PhD, David L. Delmonico, PhD, Elizabeth Griffin, MA, *In the Shadows of the Net—Breaking Free of Compulsive Sexual Behavior*, 2nd ed. (Center City, MN: Hazelden Foundation, 2007), 11. Reprinted by permission of Hazelden Foundation.

6. Dr. W. Dean Belnap, *A Brain Gone Wrong—Hope for the Troubled Teen* (Fairfax, VA: Meridian Publishing, 2008), xii.

7. Donald L. Hilton Jr., MD, *He Restoreth My Soul* (San Antonio, Texas: Forward Press, LLC, 2010), xiii.

SECTION I

PORNOGRAPHY'S DAMAGE TO THE STILL DEVELOPING BRAIN

1

THE PSYCHOLOGICAL DANGERS OF PORNOGRAPHY

Do not go gentle into that good night.
Rage, rage, against the dying of the light.

Dylan Thomas

What is one of the most powerful addictions that our youth are facing today? What "assaults the senses and manipulates the mind at both the chemical and the psychological levels" and "has the power of a heroin injection?"[1]

What gives our youth the "Triple-A Engine" effect of *accessibility*, *affordability*, and *anonymity*—a combination of traits unique to the virtual square?[2]

Additionally, what gives our youth the most perfect intense release of a "poly-drug rush," from "erototoxic stimuli,"[3] that "mimics" sexual intimacy and "fakes" the body into releasing a tidal wave of endogenous chemicals, which is exactly what pharmaceutical and illicit street drugs do[4]—leading to masturbation accompanied by orgasm (which causes the release of naturally occurring opioids)?

ONE OF THE WORST PROBLEMS
FACING PARENTS TODAY

Add to all the above, your youth can sit in the darkened privacy of their own bedrooms (illuminated only by a computer monitor or their mobile device) and link from one site to another in cyberspace, each site containing different and more erotic and hard-core images.

From his book *The Drug of the New Millennium*, Mark Kastleman shares some sobering statistics on the age group that is the largest consumer of Internet pornography: "Prior to the Internet, pornographers were almost entirely barred from a highly profitable market they desperately wanted: testosterone-saturated teenagers. Today, the largest consumers of Internet pornography are teenage boys between the ages of 12 and 17."[5]

Thanks to the uniqueness and convenience of this powerful addiction, time can actually seem to stand still for the viewer and they can be lost in a world of powerfully erotic lust for hours on end—and nobody knows. It's the most secretive and hidden of all addictions. It's pornography, and it's one of the worst problems facing parents today.

THE MORE GRAPHIC, THE MORE
ADDICTIVE IT BECOMES

Just as heroin far exceeds ordinary tobacco in its ability to produce euphoria and dependency, so the truly serious pornographers are working intensely to perfect a product that will capture an individual far more compellingly and with far greater self-destructive power than even heroin or cocaine.

The more graphic, the more powerful the vicarious experience, the more addictive it becomes.[6]

In a testimony given before a United States Senate Subcommittee in 2005, Dr. Jill Manning reported that researchers found that exposure to pornographic material puts one at increased risk for

- 31 percent increase in the risk of sexual deviancy.

- 22 percent increase in the risk of sexual perpetration.

- 20 percent increase in the risk of experiencing negative intimate relationships.

- 31 percent increase in the risk of believing rape myths.[7]

Dr. Manning further reported that "a 2002 Henry J. Kaiser Family Foundation Report found that 70 percent of youth ages 15 to 17 reported accidentally coming across pornography online, and 23 percent of those youth said this happens 'very' or 'somewhat' often. Viewers of all ages," continues Dr. Manning, "are commonly greeted with 'Click here if you are 18 years of age or older' prior to entering a sexually explicit website. However, this farcical honor system fails at protecting youth from inappropriate material because

- approximately 75 percent of pornographic websites display visual teasers on their home pages before asking if viewers are of legal age.

- only 3 percent of pornographic websites require proof of age before granting access to sexually explicit material.

- two-thirds of pornographic websites do not include adult content warnings. Although age verification measures are readily available through the use of credit cards, adult access codes, and/or personal identification numbers, the pornography industry has neglected to implement these measures even halfheartedly.

- unsuspecting youth are commonly tricked into opening pornographic websites by attaching misspelled words to pornographic sites or by making it difficult to shut down or get out of a site once opened, a strategy referred to as *mouse trapping*. In 26 percent of unwanted exposure incidents, youth reported being exposed to another sex site while they were trying to exit another."[8]

SOCIAL WORKER'S REPORT

In the many cases in which the following social worker was involved where there were complaints of sexual activity with a minor, pornography was involved:

Martha P., SSW: In my experience, regardless of whether a child was the victim of sexual abuse; an actual perpetrator of abuse; or merely sexually reactive; pornography has played a role in 100% of my sex-abuse cases. Sometimes, even in cases where the child has been taken from the environment that first exposed them to pornography and placed in foster care, the viewing of porn is so ingrained in the child that they will continue to seek it out. Time and again, foster parents find youth with some form of or access to pornography.

It is also tragic when I have found children, some as young as preschoolers, who have viewed pornography (i.e. X-rated videos or movies) sitting side by side with a parent as though they were watching Sesame Street or the Disney Channel.

Unfortunately, I'm also noticing an ever-increasing number of younger and younger perpetrators of child-on-child sexual abuse. Unlike adult perpetrators, children do not participate in sexual acts for sexual gratification. Often it is a coping mechanism for dealing with trauma, or an act of curiosity after being exposed to explicit sexual material. But regardless of the specific causal factor for each individual child, it leaves them forever altered.

Detectives Find Pictures of Children as Young as 2

A Tampa, Florida, man was arrested at his apartment earlier today after investigators say he possessed child pornography on his computer. Police say they apprehended . . . Jones, 36, after they recovered pictures of children as young as 2 and videos of children between the ages of 10 and 12 engaged in bondage and bestiality.[9]

What kind of exposure to pornography or childhood molestation was perpetrated directly on this criminal that could damage him to the point that he could be aroused by children as young as two years old?

PORN LEADS TO EARLY SEX

A website devoted to fighting pornography, cp80.org, relates several of the dangers of a youth's exposure. A new study in this month's Cyber Psychology and Behavior, a peer-reviewed journal, shows that along with alarming STD statistics, "men and women who watched pornography between the ages of 12–17 engaged in sexual behavior before others who did not."[10] The author, psychologist Shane Krauss from Castleton College in Vermont, concluded:

> Males are having oral sex and losing their virginity much younger when they are exposed to pornography, sometimes by a good three or four years for oral sex or two years for their virginity. Catherine Harper, from Scottish Women against Pornography told the Sunday Herald that venereal diseases are being spread by men asking partners to imitate what they've seen online. She said the rise in oral sex rates is linked to the highest rates in 30 years of the human papilloma virus, particularly among young men. Sue Maxwell, a psychosexual therapist, says Internet pornography adversely affects men more than women. "Instead of developing a relationship based on thinking what do you want, what do I want," she said, "[men] go for something that gives them another high, and into compulsive behavior, seeking out another sexual experience more sexually enthralling than the previous one."[11]

Science continues to catchup to common sense: pornography drives dangerous behavior.

YOUNG CHILDREN CAN GET ADDICTED

It is a fallacy that children can't get addicted to pornography. According to Dr. Donald L. Hilton Jr., young children can get addicted:

We have seen children as young as seven or eight years of age who are already addicted to pornography. Some studies show that many of those with this addiction began between the ages of five and fifteen. Some children were molested at an early age and introduced to pornography by their molester. Many have reported that as children they did not understand the powerful feelings of euphoria they experienced when viewing pornography. But later, when they were experiencing fears, sorrows, or anxieties, they would revert to viewing pornography to get those same feelings of euphoria, as a way to escape from the difficulties of life. It is important to understand that the pornography industry is targeting children to entice them into addiction.[12]

SEXUAL AGGRESSION INCREASING IN CHILDREN UNDER THE AGE OF TEN

"Childhood and adolescence," as stated by Dr. Jill Manning, "are foundational developmental stages in the formation of habits, values, attitudes, and beliefs. Children and adolescents are considered the most vulnerable audience of sexually explicit material."[13]

In recent years, an Australian Child at Risk Assessment Unit in Canberra, New South Wales, noticed a disturbing increase in the number of sexually abusive or aggressive children under the age of 10 who were being referred to their services.

To determine why this increase was occurring, the National Child Protection Clearinghouse and the Canberra Hospital conducted a retroactive study on case files. The review revealed, among other commonalities, a pattern between such sexually abusive children and their access to sexually explicit material on the Internet. "We noticed a number of really interesting issues. Of course, this primary issue is around the use of the Internet. Almost all of the children who accessed our services in the last three years in relation to sexually harmful behaviors, almost all those children had accessed the Internet and specifically had accessed the Internet for pornographic material."[14]

PORNOGRAPHY'S MASTURBATORY CONDITIONING

As presented by Dr. Victor Cline, a licensed clinical psychologist, "as a man repeatedly masturbates to a vivid sexual fantasy as his exclusive outlet, the pleasurable experiences endow the deviant fantasy (rape, molesting children, injuring one's partner while having sex, etc.) with increasing erotic value." This is one of the most personally dangerous and tragic consequences of habitual pornography viewing.[15]

An orgasm is the most "critical reinforcing event for the conditioning of the fantasy preceding or accompanying the act. Masturbatory conditioning," according to Dr. Cline, "cannot be eliminated even by massive feelings of guilt." Additionally, "the whole conditioning process and addiction can start at a very young age—as young as 8 years old."[16]

> I found that nearly all of my adult sexual addicts' problems started with porn exposure in childhood or adolescence (8 years and older). The typical pattern was exposure to mild porn early with increasing frequency of exposure and eventual later addiction. This was nearly always accompanied by masturbation.
>
> This was followed by an increasing desensitization of the materials' pathology, escalation to increasingly aberrant and varied kinds of materials, and eventually to acting out the sexual fantasies they were exposed to. While this did on occasion include incest, child molestation, and rape, most of the damage was through compulsive infidelity (often infecting the wife with Herpes or other venereal diseases) and a destruction of trust in the marital bond which in many cases led to divorce and a breaking up of the family. I found that once addicted, whether to just the pornography or the later pattern of sexual acting out, they really lost their "free agency." It was like a drug addiction. And in this case their drug was sex. They could not stop the pattern of their behavior, no matter how high-risk for them it was. In my treatment of hundreds of primarily male patients with sexual pathology (paraphilias) I have consistently found that most men are vulnerable to the effects of masturbatory conditioning to pornography with a consequence of sexual ill health, because we are

all subject to the laws of learning with few or no exceptions. In my experience as a sexual therapist, any individual is at risk of becoming, in time, a sexual addict, as well as conditioning himself into having a sexual deviancy and/or disturbing a bonded relationship with a spouse or girlfriend when this occurs.

A frequent side effect is that their capacity to love is also dramatically reduced (e.g. it results in a marked dissociation of sex from friendship, affection, caring, and other normal healthy emotions and traits which help marital relationships). This sexual side becomes, in a sense, dehumanized. Many of them develop also an "alien ego state" (or dark side), whose core is antisocial lust, devoid of most values. Raw id, in a sense. In time, the "high" obtained from masturbating to pornography *becomes more important than real life relationships.*[17]

IS PORNOGRAPHY A DRUG ADDICTION?

Dr. Randall Hyde and Dr. Bernell Christensen, who have witnessed and treated the power of pornography addiction in people's lives for a combined total of over fifty-five years, explain why pornography addiction can be labeled as a drug addiction:

> Some cringe with labeling pornography as "addictive" because they believe doing so affords the porn user an excuse: "I can't help myself, I'm addicted." This is a preposterous position. When someone is addicted to alcohol, do we excuse his behavior because "he can't help it?" Just because someone suffers with an addiction doesn't mean he doesn't have a choice. There is always a choice when it comes to breaking free from addictive behaviors. The more important question is not "Is pornography addictive?" but rather, "Is pornography a chemical addiction? Does pornography use lead to a chemical dependency commonly experienced with illicit street drugs, alcohol, and prescription drugs? Is pornography use substance abuse?" Immediately, there are some in the scientific, medical, and psychology fields who fire back, "How can you classify pornography as a drug or a substance? It doesn't come in a liquid, powder, or pill form. You don't ingest it or inject it."
>
> Our response is two-fold:
>
> 1. When an individual ingests or injects a "drug," that chemical travels to the receptors in the brain and other parts of the body,

seeking to "mimic" the body's own natural neurotransmitters. In effect, the drug "fakes" the body into releasing its own endogenous chemicals. Pornography "mimics" sexual intimacy and "fakes" the body into releasing a tidal wave of chemicals, which is exactly what pharmaceutical and illicit street drugs do. Can pornography not then be referred to as a "drug"?

2. For those who insist on precision in the use of scientific terms such as "drug," allow us to put your minds at rest. Can we agree that pornography viewing triggers the release of the body's own endogenous chemicals, just as sexual intimacy does? And that the porn viewer can become addicted to these internal chemicals just as he would if the release were triggered by a pharmaceutical drug? Is this not chemically-induced addiction?[18]

THE STORY OF SHELLEY LUBBEN, FORMER PORN STAR

The shocking knowledge of the degree of sexual violence and degradation experienced by modern-day pornography stars gives one insight into the other end of the spectrum. At the age of nine, Shelley Lubben was sexually molested. The damage done to Shelley sent her into a downward emotional and mental spiral that would turn her world into a nightmare and her life into a living hell.

The gross dichotomy of the sex industry and a lot of its porn stars (willing and unwilling) is that this life of degradation and pain is portrayed by usually drugged, sexually diseased actresses (with an abnormally young life span of 37.5 years).

Their sham of a simulation of aroused, erotic, sexual enjoyment is captured on video and film and meant to then sexually arouse and feed the appetites of individuals for their lustful "pleasure" who in the process many times ruin their own lives. In the meantime, the sex industry makes billions of dollars.

"The stars," says Shelley, "don't realize the degradation. . . . Raised on porn, [they] don't even ask if it's wrong. . . . They get into drugs to numb themselves. They get their [bodies] ripped. . . . They get HPV and herpes, and they turn themselves off emotionally and die."

Shelley says such women totally lose their identity and live on drugs and alcohol. They cannot plan, save their money, or eat properly. The survivors commonly have only sexual diseases and "fake boobs" to show for their lives in porn. She used to be one of them.

At age nine, a classmate and the girl's teenage brother sexually molested Shelley. With no one to turn to or redress her abuse, Shelley defused her anxiety via autoeroticism and furtive sexual forays with both girls and boys. "It felt good to be wanted by someone and to receive attention, but at the same time I felt dirty. I didn't recognize until much later that my entire childhood had been sexually hijacked."

Now happily married to Garrett, her husband, and the mother of three daughters, Shelley takes a message of transformation against all odds to prisons, TV, radio, film, conferences, and rescue missions. Shelley has been a guest on talk shows such as Dr. Phil, Michael Reagan, and most recently, Fox News. Her message is one of exposing the porn industry for what it is—"full of lies and deceit, addiction, and broken lives. Almost all pornography performers were sexually assaulted as children," she says, "but hide their broken hearts."

Shelley knows that porn is like any other addiction:

> First, you are curious. Then you need harder and harder drugs to get off. You need gang bangs and bestiality and child porn. Porn gets grosser and grosser.
>
> God restored me from drugs, alcohol addiction, painful memories, mental illness, sexual addiction, sexual trauma, and the guilt and shame from my past. God took me out of the old life, offered me a new life, and though I couldn't see it in the beginning, I put my hand in His and took a chance on Him. That was the best choice I ever made![19]

You can read Shelley's incredible autobiography on her website: www.shelleylubben.com.

NOTES

1. See Bobby Maddex, "The Naked Truth—An Interview with Dr. Judith Reisman," *Salvo Magazine*, http://www.drjudithreisman.com.

2. See Dr. Al Cooper, "Sexuality and the Internet—Surfing into the New Millennium," CyberPsychology & Behavior, 1998. As quoted in Jill C. Manning, MS, Submission for the Record, Testimony of Jill C. Manning. *Hearing on Pornography's Impact on Marriage & the Family,* Subcommittee on the Constitution, Civil Rights, and Property Rights Committee on Judiciary, United States Senate, November 10, 2005.

3. See Dr. Judith Reisman, "The Psychopharmacology of Pictorial Pornography/ Restructuring Brain, Mind & Memory & Subverting Freedom of Speech," White Papers, http://www.drjudithreisman.com.

4. See Dr. Randall Hyde and Mark Kastleman, "Is Pornography a Drug Addiction?" Candeocan Blog Archives (June 5, 2009), http://www.candeocan.com.

5. Kastleman, *Drug of the New Millennium*, 20.

6. John L. Harmer with James Bradford Smith, *The Sex Industrial Complex* (Salt Lake City: The Lighted Candle Society, 2007), 94.

7. Dr. Jill Manning, *Hearing on Pornography's Impact*. Bullets added.

8. Ibid. Italics and bullets added.

9   Available online at http://www.thedeadkidsofmyspace.com. Name has been changed.

10. "Porn Leads to Early Sex," CP80 News Article, 29 April 2008. Available on http://www.cp80.org.

11. Ibid.

12. Hilton, *He Restoreth My Soul*, 345.

13. Jill Manning, *Hearing on Pornography's Impact*.

14. Ibid.

15. Dr. Victor B. Cline, PhD, "Treatment and Healing of Sexual and Pornographic Addictions," Morality in Media, as quoted on http://www.obscenitycrimes.org.

16. Ibid.

17. Ibid. Italics added.

18. Dr. Randall Hyde and Dr. Bernell Christensen, "The Brain Science Behind Internet Pornography Addiction," White Papers, Jan. 2010, http://www.candeocan.com.

19. Shelley Lubben, "Shelley's Story," http://www.shelleylubben.com.

2

THE BRAIN SCIENCE OF
PORNOGRAPHY

*All healthy men, ancient and modern, Eastern and Western, know there
is a certain fury in sex that we cannot afford to inflame, and that a certain mystery and awe must ever surround it if we are to remain sane.*

G.K. Chesterton

o you "think pornography is a harmless diversion?" asks Dr.
Judith Reisman. "Think again. Exposure to provocative photographs or films—particularly when nudity is involved—has
the power of a heroin injection, as well as its toxic effects, assaulting
the senses and manipulating the mind at both the chemical and the
psychological levels."[1]

BY WHAT AGE IS THE BRAIN FULLY MATURE?

The book *The Sex Industrial Complex* says, "brain studies now
document, that the human brain does not mature until roughly age
21–25, much less the young child that believes what they see is real
(as do all our brains in fact). The difference is that children cannot
distinguish or conclude differently."[2]

In the past decade, science has determined that the brain

23

is not fully locked into patterns established or developed in early childhood. "The brain continues to develop during teen years,"[3] Dr. W. Dean Belnap, a Specialist in Pediatric and Child/ Adolescent Psychiatry, tells us as he shares his extensive knowledge of the young and still developing brain.

> Between puberty and young adulthood, the prefrontal lobe— what we call the executive portion of the brain responsible for self control, judgment, emotional regulation, organization, and planning—warps into renewed articulation. Teenage years are essentially a second chance to consolidate circuits for mature adult response. Extraneous neuro branches get pruned back as a newer and more efficient circuitry takes over.[4]

Furthermore, he writes, "teens have power over the pruning process by what they see, what they take in, what they do. It can be positive. Or negative. Teens process information differently from adults. . . . Their choices direct and give emphasis to budding interests and, hence, wire their brains for future use."[5]

Dr. Belnap calls it imprinting.

> Stamped into their minds—imprinted, is what happened today; what they saw; what they said; what they took in and what they felt.
>
> That imprinting is more than memory, more than a series of good and bad days catalogued according to date, time and place. Imprinting is a biological process that takes place in the brain where teens do their most selective thinking.[6]

REPEATED EXPOSURE TO PORNOGRAPHY AND THE YOUNG BRAIN

Would any normal, caring, parent or caregiver ignore or be unconcerned if they knew that the vulnerable and still developing brain of their child was shutting down specific functions and rewiring normal pathways, as far too many of them start a downward spiral toward pornography addiction?

Dr. Judith Reisman states that, "as far as the brain is concerned, a reward's a reward, regardless of whether it comes from a chemical or an experience. And where there's a reward, there's the risk of the vulnerable brain getting trapped in a compulsion."[7]

> When a person is exposed repeatedly to pornography the brain is stimulated and releases chemicals. This "cocktail" of chemicals builds a dependency within the brain driving feedback loops that require more and more stimulation to sustain the "high." The release of chemicals also causes the brain to shut down specific functions, rewire pathways, set expectations, and weigh decision-making in an improper way.[8]

Modern technology has provided a fascinating window through which to see actual changes and damage to the brain.

"With the aid of new technology," Dr. Belnap tells us, "sophisticated brain imaging techniques can illustrate in real-time pictures the very activation of negative imprinting from one cold beer to a joint, a violent scene played out on the big screen, a pornographic illustration on the family computer."[9]

> Initially, the stimulation tickles the brain. But for some, far too many, just that one adventure is enough to lock in an imprint that begins the downward spiral. For others long-term use cuts new pathways to the areas of the brain that control pleasure and judgment. The new routes circumvent the prefrontal lobe and response accelerates to the pleasure center. An addicted brain is both physically and chemically different from a normal brain not subjected to negative imprints. The brain has been reprogrammed to compulsively want more rather than to weigh the options.
>
> Negative imprints erode the ability to feel pleasure in those things that once produced satisfaction. Adolescents whose choices are producing negative imprints hang with others who are similar frame of mind; they share a code of secrecy. Other signals include being boldly argumentative or sullen; testy or sad; depression; showing less and less interest and motivation in school, even if grades are high; changing eating habits or not eating at all. . .
>
> Studies have shown that changes take place in the gene make-up of the brain to create temporary or permanent loss of the prefrontal

lobe of the brain. In other words, normal behavior such as loss of inhibitions, or urges to satisfy need, feed a habit or engage in violent behavior, become reality. Imprinting switches the actual DNA, turning it on and off, and in the process, changes the very essence of a teen's identity. Genes reverse when imprinted with negative experiences or behaviors. Lost are the nerve transmissions that access the unique higher centers where freedom of choice and feelings of joy are centered. Instead, once prosperous brain functions are overridden by primitive, animal-like behaviors. The result is a teen who drinks excessively, takes drugs, finds excitement in violence, seeks company with gangs, uses sex, abuses family and friends, and ultimately loses the potential to rise above self-gratification.[10]

A description and explanation of a release of neurochemicals is explained below by Doctors Randal Hyde and Bernell Christensen in their White Papers on the Brain Science of Pornography. "Pornography is powerful because it taps into intense emotional, biological and chemical connections throughout the brain and body. We have a 'built-in' sexuality and attraction. 'Pornography,'" they explain, "mimics or counterfeits" this built-in attraction. "Its goal is to ignite, excite and exploit these natural urges."[11]

These doctors use what they have termed the "Funnel of Sexual Process" as an illustration of what they feel is the most effective way to understand this process ("The Funnel" was first developed by Dr. Page Bailey and Mark Kastleman).

"THE FUNNEL"—IN A HEALTHY RELATIONSHIP VERSUS PORNOGRAPHY VIEWING

Below you will find an explanation of the Funnel of Sexual Process from two different sexual experiences—inside a healthy relationship and during pornography viewing:

Imagine in your mind an hourglass or funnel, wide at the top and slowly narrowing down to a very small passageway in the center and then back to a wide opening at the bottom. This is a perfect illustration of how the brain behaves in sexual process. In everyday life, our brain has a relatively wide perspective. But once an individual becomes sexually aroused, the brain immediately begins narrowing its focus as it releases a tidal wave of neurochemicals, culminating at climax, and then returning to its wide perspective.

Let's look at this funnel experience from two opposite vantage points—in a healthy relationship versus using pornography. In doing this, let's track just four neurochemicals released during the funnel experience.

Dopamine

First is the neurochemical dopamine. In the brain, dopamine narrowly focuses attention and energy; causes us to ignore negatives; triggers feelings of ecstasy and arousal; and creates a powerful dependency. In a healthy relationship this is a wonderful chemical because it causes the couple to focus narrowly on each other and to ignore the negatives—I can tell you that I really appreciate it when my wife's brain releases dopamine! Dopamine also creates a healthy relationship dependency.

However, move this powerful chemical into the pornography funnel and, while the process is almost identical, the outcome is radically different. The porn viewer's energy and attention are narrowly focused on the images. Any thoughts of spouse, family, beliefs, consequences, future goals, etc., are ignored and blocked out, and the release of dopamine creates a chemical dependency linked to the images that are so powerful it has been directly compared to cocaine addiction.

Norepinephrine

Next, let's look at the neurochemical norepinephrine. Whatever is being experienced when this chemical is released, the smallest details of that experience are seared in the brain as if with a branding iron. In a healthy relationship, wonderful details of the intimate experience are remembered and recalled with fondness, bringing the couple closer together. In the pornography funnel, the release of norepinephrine causes the brain to remember the smallest details of every pornographic image.

Oxytocin

The next neurochemical is known as oxytocin, the "cuddle chemical." It was first discovered flooding the brains of mothers holding their newborn child for the first time, creating a powerful bond and causing the release of milk for nursing. Oxytocin is a "bonding chemical" and is released when people hold hands, embrace, and kiss. During sexual intimacy, a tidal wave of oxytocin is released in the funnel at climax, forging a powerful bond. It's believed that when pornography viewing is coupled with sexual climax, oxytocin is released in the brain and body. However, research is beginning to suggest that the amount of oxytocin released is significantly less than what is experienced in a healthy marriage relationship. Thus, feeling lonely, disconnected, emotionally "needy," and craving "real human intimacy," an individual may seek pornography to fill these needs. But, because it's all fantasy, with no real human connection and sharing in a committed relationship, the oxytocin release is grossly insufficient and leaves the individual feeling more empty, lonely and wanting than before. Unfortunately, this only pushes many to return to the funnel through pornography, trying to fill the "hole in the soul," which of course, pornography can never accomplish.

Serotonin

And last of all, after climax, serotonin is released into the nervous system creating deep feelings of calmness, satisfaction, and release from stress. Serotonin is referred to as the "natural Prozac." Because many individuals turn to pornography as a way to self medicate and escape the trials and pressures of life, the release of serotonin is a big factor in pornography being their "drug of choice."[12]

PORNOGRAPHY'S AROUSAL COMPARES TO EXCESSIVE AMPHETAMINE USE

One of the world's leading international researchers in the field of pornography as a drug addiction is Dr. Judith Reisman. For decades, Dr. Reisman has worked closely with some of the best minds in neuroscience and neuropsychology to prove that "pornography should indeed be considered a drug, a chemical dependency, a form of substance abuse."[13]

Consider some powerful statements from Dr. Reisman and her colleagues in a widely published research paper:

Satiation effects [hours looking at Internet porn] may be compared to those related to opiate use. Fantasy behavior can be related to such neurotransmitters as dopamine, norepinephrine, or serotonin, all of which are chemically similar to the main psychedelic drugs such as LSD.

Addiction [can] exist within the body's own chemistry. Any activity that produces salient alterations in mood can lead to compulsion, loss of control, and progressively disturbed functioning.[14]

In a statement before a United States Senate Committee, Dr. Reisman testified as to the effect of pornography altering the brain:

Thanks to the latest advances in neuroscience, we now know that emotionally arousing images imprint and alter the brain, triggering an instant, involuntary, but lasting, biochemical memory trail. These media erotic fantasies become deeply imbedded, commonly coarsening, confusing, motivating, and addicting to many of those exposed.

Addiction to pornography is addiction to what I dub erototoxins—mind altering drugs produced by the viewer's own brain.[15]

Is this what we want for our children? "Erotic images physically restructure, imprint and physically damage the human brain (especially the undeveloped, juvenile brain) . . . often leading the unwary victims to join the growing epidemic of sex addition."[16]

PORNOGRAPHY IS ACTUALLY A FORM OF PRESCRIPTION DRUG ABUSE

"Why is it that some consider adrenaline and dopamine to be drugs," asks Dr. Donald L. Hilton, "if drug companies produce them, yet they will not acknowledge these same chemicals to be drugs if pornography stimulates the brain to produce them?"[17]

They are powerful endogenous (meaning our body makes them) drugs, which can actually change the physical and chemical makeup of the brain in addiction, just as they are powerful exogenous (meaning we take them into our bodies) drugs when prescribed by a doctor. The problem with pornography is that we are using adrenaline, dopamine, other powerful brain drugs without a prescription. Pornography is actually a form of prescription drug abuse when viewed in this light.[18]

"The messages of Internet pornography," as stated by Dr. Mary Anne Layden, Clinical Psychologist and Professor of Psychology in Psychiatry, "are psychologically toxic, untrue, difficult to undo and are shaped by individuals whose goals are to make money without concern for the consequences. We owe it to our youth to give them the best, protect them from the worst, and to use our wisdom, education, and experience to decide which is which."[19]

Man Pleads Guilty to Uploading Child Porn on MySpace

Texas: A 24-year-old man could face up 20 years in prison after pleading guilty to uploading child pornography on his MySpace account. [The man] told detectives that he had been collecting kiddy porn since he was 15 years old. . . . [He] used to live in an apartment next to a local elementary school, [and he] reportedly amassed at least 1,376 videos and images of children and many of them less than 12 years of age.[20]

Dr. Layden also noted that the pornographic images children receive "are permanently implanted in the brain and the unhealthy messages these images support are not easily talked away."[21]

THE CASES OF GARY BISHOP AND
TED BUNDY, SERIAL KILLERS

Another example of the effects of pornography comes from Gary Bishop, convicted homosexual pedophile who murdered five young boys in Salt Lake City, Utah, in order to conceal his sexual abuse of them. He wrote in a letter after his conviction:

> Pornography was a determining factor in my downfall. Somehow I became sexually attracted to young boys and I would fantasize about them naked. Certain bookstores offered sex education, photographic, or art books which occasionally contained pictures of nude boys. I purchased such books and used them to enhance my masturbatory fantasies.
>
> Finding and procuring sexually arousing materials became an obsession. For me, seeing pornography was lighting a fuse on a stick of dynamite. I became stimulated and had to gratify my urges or explode. All boys became mere sexual objects. My conscience was desensitized and my sexual appetite entirely controlled my actions.[22]

In the case of Ted Bundy, serial killer of possibly thirty-one young women, he stated in a videotaped interview hours before his execution: "You are going to kill me, and that will protect society from me. But out there are many, many more people who are addicted to pornography, and you are doing nothing about that."[23]

> While some commentators discounted his linking aggressive pornography to his sex-murders (even when he said it fueled his violent thoughts toward women), there seems little doubt that Bundy consumed a great deal of pornography, much of it violent, from an early age.[24]

The experts quoted in this chapter have told us why and how pornography viewing can become addictive and is especially dangerous to the still developing child's brain. For some it causes brain damage, and as stated in the quotes below, actually causes visible shrinkage in the frontal control areas.

PORNOGRAPHY ADDICTION:
A HYPOFRONTAL SYNDROME

One of the top doctors in America, Dr. Donald L. Hilton Jr., specializes in neurological surgery. He knows the brain, inside and out. He shares some of that incredible knowledge and his deep spirituality in his book *He Restoreth My Soul*.

> As a neurosurgeon, I have operated on many people through the years who have suffered traumatic brain injury from motor vehicle and other accidents, from falls, and from assaults. Tumors and other brain problems such as aneurysms can also cause similar damage. Let us consider a motor vehicle accident. With the tremendous force of deceleration suddenly stopping the skull, the brain inside the skull keeps traveling into the frontal bone [the forehead]. This produces a commonly seen finding on CT scans called a contusion, or "brain bruise." The frontal lobes of the brain swell, and the orbitofrontal, midfrontal, and other frontal areas involved in mediation and judgment of pleasure responses are damaged by the trauma and frequently become hemorrhagic [they bleed]. Sometimes this produces severe, life threatening pressure on the rest of the brain, and we must operate and remove some of the damaged frontal lobe to prevent coma and death. Upon recovery, these patients can manifest what we in neurosurgery call a "frontal lobe syndrome," or "hypofrontality." On follow-up CT scans of the brain, the frontal lobes frequently show atrophy, or shrinkage.
>
> Family members will comment that the loved one "just isn't the same." A formerly dignified and sophisticated person may be silly and may laugh or cry inappropriately and show other signs of impaired judgment. They usually manifest impulsivity or inability to prevent themselves from doing things they normally would not have done. They also exhibit compulsivity or repetition of certain behaviors they normally wouldn't be fixated on.
>
> Addiction also produces a similar hypofrontal syndrome. Prominent addiction neuroscientists describe the same behavioral findings of frontal damage in the addicted.[25]

Dr. Hilton then quotes studies that show how addictions affected the brain, including "cellular activity in the orbitofrontal cortex, a brain area we rely on to make strategic rather than impulsive, decisions. Patients with traumatic injuries to this area of the brain display problems—aggressiveness, poor judgment of future consequences, inability to inhibit inappropriate responses that are similar to those observed in substance abusers."[26]

As we conclude our education from Dr. Hilton's extensive knowledge of natural addictions and brain damage, it is comforting to know that physical damage to the brain from sex addiction can heal:

> Addiction actually causes visible shrinkage in the frontal control areas, not unlike traumatic brain injury. This has been found both in drug addictions and in natural addictions involving sexuality and overeating. Fortunately, with abstinence, there is evidence that the brain can heal and that these areas can regain their size with recovery (unlike traumatic brain injury, where the damage is more permanent). Thus addiction is literally a "collision" with the adversary producing not only a spiritual wound, but also causing physical damage to the brain. In this sense, the phrase "He Restoreth My Soul" has special relevance, as we consider that healing must address both the spirit and the body, which are the "soul of man."[27]

THE COMPUTER MONITOR
PARALLELS THE ROMAN COLOSSEUM

The history of humanity is filled with man's inhumanity to man and we find record throughout time of those who took a perverse pleasure in watching the brutalization of the innocent. The computer monitor and the TV screen have become akin to the ancient arenas, such as the Roman Colosseum, to worldwide audiences of "youth" (for the purpose of this book), where kids can participate in "funeral games" and become desensitized to the blood rites of gaming triumphs in virtual reality, or masturbate to the degenerate and dehumanizing conquests of an animal having sex with a paid porn star or an innocent child. Pornography gives them a view right into what was once the darkest brothels depicting the most sordid and perverted behavior, or to what is hideously more sadistic than the sexual torture chambers of the Marquis de Sade. For many youth, pornography viewing is an addictive, uncontrollable compulsion—a loss of control that can lead to progressively disturbed brain functioning and damage.

More and more of our youth are being drawn into it like a moth to the flame every day.

WILLIAM SHAKESPEARE: SONNET #129

The expense of spirit is a waste of shame
Is lust in action; and till action, lust
Is perjured, murderous, bloody, full of blame,
Savage, extreme, rude, cruel, not to trust;
Enjoy'd no sooner but despised straight;
Past reason hunted; and no sooner had,
Past reason hated, as a swallowed bait,
On purpose laid to make the taker mad:
Mad in pursuit, and in possession so;
Had, having, and in quest to have, extreme;
A bliss in proof, and proved, a very woe;
Before, a joy proposed; behind, a dream.
All this the world well knows; yet none knows well
To shun the heaven that leads men to this hell.

NOTES

1. See Maddex, "The Naked Truth," http:// www.drjudithreisman.com
2. Harmer and Smith, *The Sex Industrial Complex*, 228.
3. Belnap, *A Brain Gone Wrong*, 3.
4. Ibid.
5. Ibid.
6. Ibid.
7. Reisman, "The Psychopharmacology of Pictorial Pornography," White Papers, http://www.drjudithreisman.com.
8. Ibid.

9. See Belnap, *A Brain Gone Wrong,* 5.

10. Ibid., 5–6.

11. See Hyde and Christensen, "The Brain Science Behind Internet Pornography Addiction," available at http://www.candeocan.com.

12. Ibid.

13. Reisman, "The Psychopharmacology of Pictorial Pornography," White Papers, http://www.drjudithreisman.com.

14. Ibid.

15. Dr. Judith Reisman Testimony, Senate Committee on Commerce, Science, Transportation, Witness List, *Hearing on the Brain Science Behind Pornography Addiction and the Effects of Addiction on Families and Communities,* November 18, 2004. Available online at http://www.obscenitycrimes.org.

16. Harmer and Smith, *The Sex Industrial Complex,* 211.

17. Hilton, *He Restoreth My Soul,* 53.

18. Ibid., 53–54.

19. See Dr. Mary Anne Layden, as quoted in "Why Do Kids Encounter Online Pornography? Because Obscenity Laws Aren't Enforced," htpp://www.obscenitycrimes.org.

20. Available online at www.thedeadkidsofmyspace.com, name withheld.

21. Layden, "Why Do Kids Encounter Online Pornography?" htpp://www.obscenitycrimes.org.

22. Victor B. Cline, PhD, "Pornography's Effects on Adults and Children," quoted in "The Porn Problems and Solutions," http://www.obscenitycrimes.org.

23. Ibid.

24. Ibid.

25. Hilton, *He Restoreth My Soul,* 52.

26. Joanna L. Fowler, Nora D. Volkow, Cheryl A. Kassed, and Linda Chang, *Imaging the Addicted Human Brain,* as quoted by Hilton, *He Restoreth My Soul,* 52–53.

27. Hilton, *He Restoreth My Soul,* 52–53

3

CHILD
PREDATORS

Man is the most formidable of all beasts of prey, and, indeed, the only one that preys systematically on its own species.

WILLIAM JAMES

"New brain imaging surveys and other experiments have shown that child abuse can cause permanent damage to the neural structure and function of the developing brain itself (if the abuse is not recognized and/or treated successfully). These grim results suggest that much more effort must be made to prevent childhood abuse and neglect before it does irrevocable harm to millions of young victims."[1]

THE WORST AND MOST DAMAGING FORM OF CHILD ABUSE

The damage done to children who are sexually abused, exploited in child pornography, or prostituted in child sex trafficking, is the worst and most damaging form of child abuse and victimization. In addition, as mentioned previously, the harm done to the developing brains of children who view pornography is a form of child abuse.

According to the National Society for the Prevention of Cruelty to Children, "there are more than 20,000 images of child pornography posted online every week, and 100,000 websites offer illegal child pornography."[2]

These websites are prowled over, lusted over, and shared between the most perverted and evil of all predators—a pedophile, who can act out on his perversion and molest a child. There is no statistic that could ever measure the amount of fear and pain that they have inflicted and continue to inflict upon our young ones.

"Demand for pornographic images of babies and toddlers on the Internet is soaring. It is more torturous and sadistic than it was before. The typical age of children is between six and twelve, but the profile is getting younger."[3]

The availability of child pornography is fueling the age-old pedophile cravings that might not have been acted upon.

Springfield, MA: Springfield businessman, indicted on federal charges for advertising, possession, and distribution of child porn. He shared 313 images with an undercover FBI agent while using the screen name "Like22look." The ages of the children were 1 to 5, shown engaging in sadistic sexual acts with adults. He advertised on a P2P file sharing program seeking to buy, sell, and trade images of children engaged in sexual acts. If convicted, he faces a prison sentence between 15–30 years for each advertising charge, 5–10 years for each distribution charge, and up to 10 years for each possession charge.[4]

TESTIMONY OF A CALIFORNIA DETECTIVE

On February 10, 1998, the United States Senate Commerce Subcommittee with jurisdiction over communications received the following testimony from Detective Daryk Rowland:

> My name is Daryk Rowland. I am a detective with the Huntington Beach, California, Police Department and a member of the Southern California Regional S.A.F.E. Team. One of my assignments is to monitor and investigate criminal activity occurring on the Internet, especially those crimes dealing with child pornography and child sexual exploitation. I have participated in numerous cases which resulted in the arrest and conviction of child molesters who contacted their child victims on the Internet on-line services.
>
> My purpose today is to communicate with you the immense danger that exists for children from sexual predators and from hard-core adult and child pornography available on the Internet to children by their personal and school computers.
>
> Because of unfiltered or unsupervised access to the Internet and on-line services, children are being enticed and lured away from home, sexually molested, and victimized through the distribution of child pornography.
>
> With a simple floppy disc inserted into a school computer, a child can run a program that will allow him to access the Internet Relay Chat. From there students have access to thousands of pornographic images and the ability to have conversations with strangers that would otherwise not occur. Students can access free, personal, anonymous email accounts from school and converse instantly with strangers they meet on the Internet. There are also several programs available that can tell a child when someone he has met on the Internet is on line and available to chat. All of these programs can operate on a computer at home or school.
>
> Sexual predators who want to molest children have learned very fast how to communicate with and lure children. They are feeling much safer in their own homes to contact children by computer. They no longer have to wait at the shopping mall or near a park or school, and they can do it any time of the day or night. All they need is Internet access or an on-line service to begin to contact children.[5]

"Detective Rowland's testimony was an incredible litany of specific examples of how children and young teenagers were lured into sexual molestation after being allowed to engage in unsupervised 'chat room' activity on the family computer. He then went on to point out that far too often the users of the Internet at schools have no supervision whatsoever, or very passive irresponsible supervision. All of this, he asserted, leads to a high possibility for tragedy in the lives of thousands of young people."[6]

PROFILE OF A PEDOPHILE

A pedophile is an individual whose perversion has created within him or her a craving for sexual involvement with children (which includes infants).

From their book *In the Shadows of the Net—Breaking Free from Online Sexual Behavior*, Dr. Patrick Carnes, Dr. David L. Delmonico, and Elizabeth Griffin, MA (experts in online compulsive sexual behavior) tell us about the arousal patterns of pedophiles.

> Pedophiles, people who were severely damaged as children and who, as a result, have rigid arousal templates that deviated dramatically from normal behavior. (You have an arousal template that is essentially a pattern you created unconsciously as you were growing up—one that determines what you find sexually arousing— whether or not you are not aware of its existence.[7]) It is extremely difficult for these people to make significant changes in their arousal templates because the damage they suffered is so deep and came so early in life. Their behavior has been in a set groove for a long time.[8]

Pedophiles can be treated but never cured because their sexual preference will always be children.

There are "exclusive pedophiles," who are attracted to children only—but be forewarned that there is such a thing as the classification of "nonexclusive pedophile"—those who are sexually attracted to adults as well as children.

A pedophile can be a heterosexual, a homosexual, or a bisexual.

PEDOPHILIA

Pedophilia is the form of pornography that exhibits children, sometimes infants, in sexually explicit conduct.

> It is difficult for those who have never seen this material to comprehend how vile, how perverted, and how repulsive to any sense of dignity or civility it is. Child pornography, or pedophilia, has become rampant throughout the world as pornography addicts become obsessed with this depravity. In recent years individuals from every walk of life, from university presidents and members of congress, to school principals, priests, and ministers of religions, have been arrested, tried, and convicted for the crime of producing and distributing child pornography or pedophilia.[9]

WHEN THE PEDOPHILE IS SOMEONE THEY KNOW

Milford, MA: An 18-year-old teen has been arrested for forcible rape of a 5-year-old boy he was babysitting. According to the criminal complaint filed, he admitted to detectives that he forced the boy to perform oral sex on him. Authorities decline to say how long the abuse lasted. The alleged victim told a team of investigators, which included detectives and assistant district attorneys, that he didn't want to do what [the teen] said. "I told him it was yucky but he said no, it's not yucky," the boy said, according to the complaint filed. . . . [The suspect] is being held at the Worcester County House of Correction on a $50,000 cash bail. He is facing 10 years to life in state prison if convicted of raping a child by force. He is also charged with indecent assault and battery on a child under 14.[10]

Equally vital is educating your children on personal boundaries with those that they know—a favorite babysitter or family member or friend. Tell your child in age-appropriate language that behavior from anyone—family members, friends, babysitters, neighbors, and so on—that scares him, makes him feel uncomfortable, invades his privacy or personal body areas (or if he is asked to touch other people's private body areas) is not acceptable, and it is important for him to stand up for himself by saying "no," getting away from that person, and telling you immediately. Make sure your child knows that even if a molester has threatened him or someone he loves that you will always protect him.

The nature of these sorts of conversations may be one that you've never considered even approaching before with your child, especially a young child; however, now is the time. Sexual perversions are being fueled by pornography. More and more pedophiles are acting out their heretofore secret cravings. The properly prepared child is a safer child.

Never force your child to sit on the lap, kiss, hug, or touch anyone she does not wish to, even if it's a relative. Even though this might seem rude to you, this gives a child a sense of empowerment and teaches her that she can say no to unwanted contact.

Additionally, make sure your child knows about "secrets." Secrets are only for Christmas presents or birthday surprises. Teach your child that it is not right for an adult to ask her to keep a kiss or a touch secret.

All of the above can be taught to a child in a nonthreatening, calm, and resolute manner.

However, this can be very difficult for children if the pedophile is a beloved family member. The inconceivable sexual molestation of a child by his own parent can cause horrible trauma to a child. In cases such as these, children will feel a myriad of powerful, conflicting emotions that most likely will traumatize and damage them for their entire lives, affecting their relationships with their own children and sometimes leaving them with a disposition toward being the perpetrators of the same abusive behavior.

If communication channels are kept open with your children it is easier to initiate discussions with them if they are displaying any of the warning signs of sexual molestation. Remember, little ones very seldom lie about inappropriate sexual contact, and their concerns should be respected. The sooner sexual molestation is stopped and dealt with, the better a child's chances are of beginning the healing process (see chapter 11 on Communicating with Your Child).

It is a tragic fact that the emotional and mental damage done to a child by sexual abuse during childhood can be irreversible and plague her for her entire life if not property treated. The abuse can lead to a variety of mental problems, including out of control and personally damaging sexual behaviors, sexual perversions, unfulfilling sexual addiction, depression, alcohol or drug abuse, anxiety disorders, and so on. Some, but not all abused children, go on to become pedophiles themselves; however, there is no pedophile gene. It is not genetic—it is an acquired perversion, and if the perversion seems to run in families, one has to take into account that the aforementioned victimization of a child might cause that child to continue the chain of abusive behavior as he matures.

INCEST

According to the experts, a pedophile will typically not stop his behavior on his own, he will certainly not turn himself in, and most times he will not even take responsibility or even admit any wrongdoing. This can be especially true if the molester is the child's father or close relative. For example, if an uncle is tucking your child into bed on a regular basis or has an unusually close relationship with young ones, this should set up warning flags, and you should investigate.

One young woman related that her thirty-year-old brother-in-law (she was twelve at the time) got her alone one day at her home, took her into a bedroom, and sexually attacked her. Afterwards, she scrubbed herself in the bathtub for hours, and in her trauma and disgust ate most of a bar of soap. Her parents and sister believed her, and the predator was ostracized from the family; however, they were too protective of their family image to initiate charges against him, thereby guaranteeing that she did not have access to therapy and those who knew how to help her heal.

In her shame, self-blame, and emotional trauma, she went on to become an extremely sexually needy teen who could never find love and fulfillment and was even raped several times more. She has struggled through one destructive marriage and now is trying to be a good mother and nurture another relationship. She does face the fears that she might someday do something to one of her own children, probably a common fear of sexual victims but one that hugely takes away from her joy and self-esteem.

Concerning a child's own father—this unthinkable victimization happens more that you can even begin to imagine. One anonymous victim related than her father had sexually abused not only her but also her sisters. Her father was a pillar of the community, a religious leader, and a well-respected man. Ironically, he was a licensed therapist, counseling children, couples, and families. One of her now grown sisters, who took the worst of the abuse, is a drug and sex addict who has tried to commit suicide several times.

The way her mother dealt with what she knew was obviously going on under her own roof was *not* to deal with it. She emotionally turned herself off and pretended nothing wrong was happening. The father wasn't confronted until years later, at which time he said that anything he might have done that was out of line was in the past, and it was something he would never even consider doing again. He is now divorced and married to another woman and has grandchildren of his own that he has access to. Their parents think he is a wonderful man and have no problem leaving their children with him.

A middle-aged man (again one who wishes to stay anonymous) related that he had been molested by his father at a young age. He tried to internalize the trauma, but it stayed with him his entire life. He married and had children but was unable to maintain a normal, loving, and affectionate relationship with his own children. His overwhelming fear was that if he allowed himself to become physically and emotionally affectionate with his children that he might let loose some monster hiding within him that would harm his children. His children grew up resenting this cold shell of a father. Now in therapy as an adult, he has been able to heal to the point where he can try to establish a relationship with his now-grown children and also deal with the ugliness of his childhood abuse.

If a father is sexually molesting his children, there are sometimes signs—the dad who loves to take baths or showers with his kids or bathe them after they have reached an inappropriate age. The father who likes to climb "under the covers" with his children and have "sleep nights" or "TV nights" on a regular basis. Or the father who takes more than the usual nude pictures of his children—especially when the shots always seem to have their genitals showing.

Then there's the man who marries a divorced woman and becomes exceptionally close to her kids and desires regular alone time with them. Perhaps child pornography shows up on the computer's browser history (this can also be a warning sign that there is a perpetrating sibling in the household).

In some cases, a man who is on the sex offender registry marries a woman who is longing for a relationship and then provides him access to a child. No woman should leave a child with a known pedophile, even if he told her "he's not aroused by children anymore." Or sometimes a person simply marries a rotten egg and keeps her mouth shut for fear of retaliation or losing her breadwinner.

Admittedly, some vicious women lie about these sorts of behaviors when an ugly divorce is unfolding just to get the man in trouble and keep him from the children. Certainly all of these things have to be thought through. A mother has to put her own needs aside and think of her child first.

Remember, a true pedophile rarely can be cured of his condition, and the child must be the priority.

Pedophiles can be some of the most cunning and charming people to be around. They are known for courting lonely single mothers just to get at their children. They like to be around children and will take the child under their wing and offer help with rides and babysitting.

Sometimes, to the extreme detriment of innocent children, a woman will condone or even join with her husband in the abuse of their children.

An Oregon couple have been arrested after they admitted to police that they sexually assaulted and then photographed two of their own children, according to a report. . . . Upon further questioning, the couple then admitted that they also had been making their own kiddy porn pictures to add to their collection. The alleged photos in question were reportedly of themselves molesting two of [their] own children that were ultimately uploaded on their personal computer and saved for future viewing, among other things.[11]

ERIN RUNNION—A WARNING
FROM AN ABDUCTED CHILD'S MOTHER

The following message on pedophiles comes from Erin Runnion, the founder of the Joyful Child Foundation, and the mother of Samantha (the little girl this book is dedicated to).

A Warning From Erin Runnion

A study done a few years ago regarding possessors of child pornography found 80 percent had images of children ages 6–12; 19 percent had images of infants and toddlers; 83 percent had images of rape; 21 percent had images of sadistic abuse and torture; 1 percent limited their "collections" to images of nude children (not being obviously abused).

As frightening as it is to realize that there are at least one million individuals who find these horrific images and videos entertaining, it is equally frightening to imagine the countless young people growing up with easy access to these images and videos.

Perpetrators can now go on the Internet and find fuel for their sick fantasies, and worse yet, they find a community of predators online seeking to justify and assist one another's criminal behavior. The man who abducted, raped, and murdered Samantha did in fact have child pornography on his computer. He was also engaging in online conversations with other predators about someday having his own children who he could molest and use to get access to other kids. Sadly, he was pretty typical for a child molester. Everything he did was designed to help him get alone time with little girls.

Long before the man who killed Samantha became the horror that he is now, he was a common child molester. That is to say, that what happened to Samantha was an extreme case of a painfully common problem. The man who killed Samantha had been accused and tried for molesting two girls (one his girlfriend's daughter and the other, her cousin). We now know that there were at least two other victims as well. He preyed on women who were vulnerable, who were overwhelmed by the responsibilities of single motherhood. He made himself a friend, someone they could count on, who would listen. He adored their children and bought them presents and took them to fun places. He got to where they trusted him to be alone with their children. All the while he was testing boundaries and breaking them—one tickle, bath, and bedtime kiss at a time. He won Mommy's trust so that the little girls' came easily. His victims were all between six and nine. To this point, he was just like hundreds of thousands of other pedophiles (not just those who have been caught and registered). He went through life behaving as though he was a good-hearted, reliable kind of guy so even though he was awkward and maybe a little creepy, one could only point to those nice things he did.

STRANGER DANGER

With the increase in child predators seeking out young victims, parents need to initiate situational education to include "what if" practice drills for children of all ages—whether it's what to do at the store, in the park, walking to the corner store or school, or even playing in their own front yard. Children need to know that appropriate strangers—store clerks or police officers—can offer assistance if they are lost or need help. The idea is not to scare children, but because children are naïve and trusting by nature, they need to be made aware of "stranger danger" through some sample role-playing. This has to be a repeated educational activity for all children, including teens.

It is also important to remember that the majority of people who like and work with children are not pedophiles.

Keep in mind that "two in five abductions of children ages 15–17 years old are due to Internet connections."[12]

WHAT TO DO IF YOU SUSPECT YOUR CHILD HAS BEEN SEXUALLY MOLESTED

One of the worst nightmares for parents is the sexual molestation of their child. If you suspect or if your child discloses sexual molestation, how you react can not only influence the future healing process (or further trauma) of the child but also affect the resultant legal proceedings that will (and have to) ensue and how your child will react to the investigative process. Remember, a child will rarely lie about sexual molestation.

It is imperative that you don't minimize what has happened to your child but at the same time stay calm (do not panic), and respect either your child's decision to talk to you or her inability to discuss anything.

Make sure your child knows that you love her, that she has done nothing wrong, that she is a victim, and that it was the perpetrator's fault—not hers. Do not blame the child. Do not demand details. Do respect her privacy when it comes to who in the family will be told what happened to her and who will not.

You must

- Get medical attention for your child.

- Notify law enforcement.

- Call the Child Abuse Hotline (the phone number is in the front of your phone book), or call 411 and get the number. This will start you on the road to alerting youth-services and appropriate social-service organizations in cooperation with law enforcement who will not only start your child on the road to therapy, but initiate action against those who abused your child.

CYBERTIPLINE

The Congressionally mandated CyberTipline is a means for reporting crimes against children including:

- Possession, manufacture, and distribution of child pornography

- Online enticement of children for sexual acts

- Child prostitution

- Sex tourism involving children

- Extrafamilial child sexual molestation

- Unsolicited obscene material sent to a child

- Misleading domain names

- Misleading words or digital images on the Internet

Reports may be made twenty-four hours a day, seven days a week online at www.cybertipline.com or by calling 1-800-843-5678.

CHILD TRAFFICKING AND PROSTITUTION

All of the various avenues through which child predators victimize and torture children are especially heinous and incomprehensible—especially child prostitution. It is a despicably big business in foreign countries but also a growing problem in the United States, as the CP80 Foundation reports to us:

"Sex Culture Fueling Child Prostitution: Last month the San Jose Mercury News reported that San Jose police identified at least 293 teens being prostituted in 2003."[13] This is an older statistic. The problem has been growing and spreading like a cancerous growth since then.

The increase in children entering the sex industry has led police to change how they deal with this problem. Officers are being trained to identify and understand physical and sexual abuse, and are treating these children as victims, rather than criminals. The Internet has made it easier for children to be used and abused as pimps can put up ads online.

Former federal prosecutor Pat Trueman says the availability of pornography online is fueling the problem. "What you're finding in today's society is a greater interest in illicit sex than ever before," explains Trueman. "The Internet has caused that because an individual can go on the Internet, see hard-core pornography, see child pornography, and have almost zero chance of being caught. The next thing they want to do, then, is have sex with a child prostitute."[14]

"An estimated 325,000 United States children age 17 or younger are prostitute performers in pornographic videos."[15]

One of the vilest global tragedies happening today is the worldwide epidemic of illicit child trafficking. The Internet is the cyberspace pimp that plays a huge role in the advertising and trafficking of child sex slaves.

NOTES

1. Reisman, "The Psychopharmacology of Pictorial Pornography," White Papers.
2. National Society for the Prevention of Cruelty to Children, 8 Oct. 2003, as quoted in "The Ugly Statistics/The Porn Stats," The Lighted Candle Society, http://www.lightedcandle.org.
3. Kastleman, *The Drug of the New Millennium*, 9.
4. http://www.thedeadkidsofmyspace.blogspot.com, May 2008. Name changed.
5. Quoted in Harmer and Smith, *The Sex Industrial Complex*, 87, 88.
6. Harmer and Smith, *The Sex Industrial Complex*, 88
7. Carnes, *In the Shadows of the Net*, 59.
8. Ibid., 65.
9. Harmer and Smith, *The Sex Industrial Complex*, 26.
10. http://thedeadkidsofmyspace.com
11. Harmer and Smith, *The Sex Industrial Complex*, 26.
12. "The Ugly Statistics/The Porn Stats," http://www.lightedcandle.org.
13. "Sex Culture Fueling Child Prostitution," CP80 News, http://www.cp80.org, accessed 5 May 2008.
14. Ibid.
15. Kastleman, *The Drug of the New Millennium*, 9.

SECTION II

THE LIMITLESS BOUNDARIES
OF CYBERSPACE

4

THE INTERNET

In 1993, when internet pornography became public, there was this huge cultural shift, and the protective barrier between the sex industry and youth dissolved. What used to be difficult for youth to access had suddenly become amazingly easy.

Jill Manning, PhD

THE MORE BIZARRE THE VISUAL IMAGE
THE MORE LIKELY WE ARE TO REMEMBER IT

Susan Baily, professor of child and adolescent forensic mental health (London), believes that it is important for parents to monitor what images their children are exposed to, especially with the increasing number of TV and computer screens in most homes. She says: "The work I have done on children who have killed, committed sexual offenses, or other crimes suggest that exposure to pornography is a factor. It is certainly well documented in the literature. You find that they model themselves on what they've seen."[1]

"Sight is the most likely to involve recall, and the more bizarre the visual image the more likely we are to see and remember it, even if not in conscious memory."[2]

A PUBLIC HEALTH EMERGENCY

Many individuals fight against the evils of pornography—they are aware of the powerful and amazing influence of the Internet and devote their time and money getting involved in the conflict against pornography found therein. Ralph Yarro, a former Novell executive, is now a self-funded computer entrepreneur who devotes his time to fighting pornography. He describes the current situation as "a public health emergency with the most addictive substance on the face of the earth. It is morally degrading beyond anything we've seen in history. . . . Wake up!" Yarro says, "Apathy will kill you here. If porn hasn't touched your life already, it is going to rip huge, gaping holes in it. You better get active real quick."[3]

A 21-year-old Ohio woman is scheduled to appear in court later today on charges of possessing and distributing child pornography over the Internet. [She] was originally arrested back in November in a major six-month-long sting, known as Operation SafetyNet. [She] is believed to have downloaded at least 17 photos and shared a total of 66 online. Most of the pictures featured infants and bestiality, prosecutors say. Besides the MySpace profile, she marked her spots online at both Blackplanet and Cutemeter. On the latter she states her age as 17; however, it could be an older account as well. [She] does have another photo bucket with over 150 different images.[4]

"The Internet just scares us to death," says David Flowers, concerning the flood of online porn. "Flowers is a 28-year veteran with the Utah Division of Youth Corrections. . . . Flowers, who has focused his work on juvenile sex offenders, says he is already beginning to see the edge of a disturbing trend with more teenagers regularly talking about such perversions as necrophilia, bestiality, and ritualistic mutilation."[5]

And this is with juveniles? No wonder David Flowers is "scared to death" by the Internet.

From the book *In the Shadows of the Net*, we read: "Some live video sites accept requests for specific sexual behaviors from online users, thus enabling individuals to create and fulfill personal fantasies."[6] Thanks to live video feed technology:

> . . . it is even possible to chat online while viewing pornography. Such virtual video booths are steadily growing in number and allow cybersex users to have nearly complete control over the "object" at the other end of the phone line even though the "object" happens to be a human being.[7]

Dr. David Delmonico, PhD, is the Director of the Online Behavior Research and Education Center at Duquesne University. He noted the "increasing problems of teenagers and even eleven-year-olds who appear to be in need of therapy for depression when in fact they are in the early stages of pornography addiction."[8]

"Cybersex activity," as quoted from Dr. Delmonico, "includes problems that involve viewing, creating, and involvement in progressively more violent forms of pornography. He confirmed the significant increase in sexualized gaming, sex chat conversations, sexual texting by teenagers using cell phones and other mobile devices."[9]

"I'm very concerned about children," Donna Woods of the University of Michigan said at an annual meeting of the American Psychiatric Association, adding that "easily accessed pornography was portraying sex as a public event, disconnected from commitment. It also offers a smorgasbord of aberrant behavior. . . . There is going to be a big public health issue." She said she had "treated a teenage boy who had become a zoophile through various websites that caused him to spend 16 hours a day on the Internet without eating or bathing."[10]

Dr. Victor Cline has "treated boys in their early teens getting into this wasteland with disastrous consequences. They told me they actively search for porn on the Internet, keying in on such words as sex, nudity, obscenity, pornography, etc. Then, once they have found how to access it, they go back again and again, just like drug addicts."[11]

Fort Knox, KY: Army Soldier, 36, and his live-in girl-friend, were arrested for amassing 2,371 images/videos of child porn on their home computer. [The soldier,] who works in the Army Recruiting Command at Fort Knox, thought his computer had a virus. He took it to the base tech department to get it fixed. During repair, very, very graphic images of seven- and eight-year-old children were discovered by techies. The images and videos depicted children being sexually assaulted. Some of the victims have been identified by the Center for Missing and Exploited Children. The woman told authorities that she accidentally came across the images and videos while googling "child porn," and that she didn't download any of them. They have been arrested and charged with felony possession of matter portraying minors in a sexual performance. More charges are expected as the case will be handed over to the grand jury. They both remain in jail on $15,000 bonds.[12]

I WISH I COULD SCRUB THE FILTH
OF THE MEMORY FROM MY BRAIN

On Saturday, January 6, 2007, the Lighted Candle Society received a report from one of the most noted authorities on the use of the Internet by pornographers, Lt. Col. Dave Grossman, US Army (Ret). Col. Grossman is the Director of the Killology Research Group, a West Point psychology professor, and an internationally recognized scholar, author, soldier, and speaker. He is one of the world's foremost experts in the field of human aggression and the roots of violence and violent crime.

"At our request," the Lighted Candle Society reported, "Col. Grossman did an analysis of the current content of child pornography on the Internet. As an experienced expert on the extent of graphic presentations of vile materials, Col. Grossman was deeply stunned at how much worse the content of the child pornography type material on the Internet had become. Here are some excerpts from his report that we received on 6 January 2007:"[13]

> Things have gone vastly, stunningly downhill. It was like descending thru Dante's layers of hell, each layer more disgusting than the next. I thought there would be a lot of "virtual child porn" since the Supreme Court had opened the door for that one. And there was some, but it was surprisingly little and hard to access without spending money and joining a service. Then I found out why there was so little of the virtual child porn: why make the effort to create the stuff, when the real thing is available so widely and openly?
>
> First there was a layer of dozens of sites with a kind of "plausible deniability." . . . they had some young teens mixed in with young looking but probably adult girls. But all you had to do was follow the "incest links" and you came to pages with clearly preteen girls.
>
> Again, all you had to do was click on the pictures of preteen girls and you could find pages and pages of such sites, with nude preteens. Years ago, last time I looked, there was some of these, but you had to join a pay site to really get any quantity. Now it is available in vast amounts to any pervert who can click a picture. But if you clicked just a little more, you could find pages and pages of the vilest, sickest, most depraved stuff. . . .

I've seen a lot of bad things in my life. Dead bodies. Dead kids. The worst things in many foreign lands and war zones. But I've never seen anything like this. Babies being abused. I can't get it out of my mind. I had nightmares about it and I wish I could scrub the filth of the memory from my brain. The bad part was that there is so VERY much of it. Again, pages and pages. (I really don't remember any of the web sites' names and have tried to flush them from my memory.) What is going to come of all this? I am a guy who thinks in historical terms, and history has a way of swinging to extremes.[14]

A GROWING PROBLEM AMONG FEMALES

Even though most addicts are male, don't neglect educating your girls. It's a growing problem among females, especially in chat rooms.

Let's look at some statistics about women and pornography:

- Women keeping their cyber activities secret—70%

- Ratio of women to men favoring chat rooms—2X

- Women accessing adult websites each month—9.4 million

- Women admitting to accessing pornography at work—13%[15]

- More than 80% of women who suffer with this addiction take it offline. Women, far more than men, are likely to act out their behaviors in real life, such as having multiple partners, engaging in casual sex, or entering into affairs.[16]

As found in CP80's News Articles, a new book says there is a growing female audience for Internet pornography.

> Australian author Catharine Lumby told *The Daily Telegraph* that her book, *The Porn Report*, breaks down several myths about pornography and women. "One of the myths (about pornography) suggests that women aren't consumers but we have very clear evidence that there's a growing proportion of porn consumers who are women," she said. "The statistics are so high now that that myth doesn't seem correct."

Ms. Lumby conducted the study over three years. Her research showed that although men still outnumber women 4 to 1 as porn consumers, the difference is getting smaller. She also noted the growing trend of homemade pornography. More and more women are creating and posting their own pornography on the Internet.[17]

Many times we associate pornography viewing with the male gender, but there are many females who are weighed down with the same addiction.

How does pornography affect females? There are women who are sex addicts and porn addicts. There are female pedophiles who molest children. The same problems exist for females who are caught in the world of addiction.

- 28% of those admitting to sexual addiction are women

- 43% of American women suffer from Female Sexual Dysfunction

- 34% of female readers of Today's Christian Woman's online newsletter admitted to intentionally accessing Internet porn in a recent poll and 1 out of every 6 women struggles with an addiction to pornography.[18]

Most certainly, you have to factor in chat rooms, social networking, and sexting. Females are especially social and sometimes needy by nature and are participating in these Internet and mobile device activities at a younger and more alarming rate. Females are more apt to gravitate to reading pornography in the form of text than their male counterparts who are more aroused by visual images. They are also more prolific in sexting out explicit photos of themselves. Another facet of the importance of educating young females is that they need to be prepared to deal with the consequences of a male's attempt to mirror viewed pornography acts upon young girls.

> Texas: A 29-year-old woman has been jailed on a $125,000 bond after she allegedly sent an undercover detective more than 100 pictures of children engaged in sexual activity. The suspect was taken into custody on Thursday after police confiscated several computers, DVDs, and pictures the previous night. Investigators working the case say that it appears that the woman might have even taken some of the pictures herself. The images of the children are believed to be both boys and girls from pre-school to pre-teen. She currently remains at the county jail.[20]

CHAT ROOMS—THE PLAYGROUND OF THE PEDOPHILE

Statistics show that "50% of high school students 'talk' in chat rooms or use instant messaging (IM) with Internet strangers."[19]

The "chat room" is one facet of Internet use that many parents do not even realize exists. In the chat room individuals type instant messages back and forth to each other in real time over the Internet—but it's like being on an old-fashioned party line: everyone in the chat room can see what you're typing. It can let you have a conversation with a neighbor who lives on the other side of your fence or a stranger on the other side of the world.

A survey showed that "86% of girls polled said they could chat online without their parents' knowledge and 54% could conduct a cyber relationship."[21] Chat rooms allow predators to pose as understanding, new best friends. They also allow participants to go off onto private chat areas. The chat room is the target of choice for the pedophile, who is constantly looking for the opportunity to persuade a young user to agree to a secret meeting. Youth of all ages should not be allowed into chat room sites.

"MOUSE TRAPPED"—HOW TO EXIT
A PORN SITE

When you've become educated on the threat of the pornography being viewed by our youth on the Internet, it should "scare us all to death." Let's re-emphasize that one of the most immediate and vital tools is to make sure your children know how to exit inappropriate websites. In the time it takes for them to repeatedly try to exit a pornography teaser site that had caught them by surprise and "mouse trapped" them, they were probably deluged with one vile and shocking picture after another. Even if you have good parent/child communication and rules, and parental controls and filters (actually filters aren't foolproof), they could click onto a site that may have a built-in program that keeps looping back after you try to exit, time and time again. In that short amount of time as they try to exit, the vilest of images can be permanently imprinted into their memory.

Some kids are disgusted with the pornographic images they're viewing and might continue to view the images out of a morbid fascination or until they figure out how to escape the site and don't desire to repeat the experience again. One ten-year-old girl thoroughly examined page after page in horror and disgust, followed by guilt. She felt no desire whatsoever to view pornography again but didn't tell an adult for months because she was afraid she'd get in trouble for not turning it off sooner. (See chapter 11, Communication with Your Child.) She lives with what she says are, "the disgusting pictures stuck in my mind."

However, some kids don't even try to exit because they are literally trapped in a world of morbid fascination as they continue to examine each shocking image. These are the kids that are most likely to seek out pornography again and again. Their brains have just been delivered a cocktail of powerful brain chemicals. Some eventually become desensitized to the deviate nature of what they are viewing and seek out more graphic and stimulating porn accompanied by self-gratification. What was at first shocking to them becomes compulsively addictive.

The safest strategy is to communicate with and educate your children—before they are faced with this type of situation. *Teach them to simply and immediately turn off their computer or walk away from any computer or device that's displaying porn.* It's a very simple, defensive tactic.

A PUBLIC HEALTH PROBLEM THAT IS SPIRALING OUT OF CONTROL

"Dr. Jerald Block, a psychiatrist at the Oregon University in Portland, says that Internet addiction should be included in the Diagnostic and Statistical Manual of Mental Disorders, the profession's official manual."[22] In a CP80 news article, Dr. Block pointed out:

> South Korea considers Internet addiction one of its most serious public health issues. At least 10 people in South Korea died from blood clots that developed after they remained sitting for long periods of time in Internet cafes. The South Korean government estimates that 210,000 children are affected; 80% of them need drugs targeting the brain and 25% would need to go to the hospital. Reports from China indicate that as many as 10 million young people are suffering from Internet addiction.
>
> The article also quotes the Pennsylvania-based Centre for Internet Addiction Recovery which says that Internet addiction is a growing criminal, divorce, and employment problem. The center offers consultations to lawyers who are "assessing the role of electronic anonymity in the development of deviant, deceptive and illegal sexual online activities."
>
> Clearly concerns about Internet and pornography addiction are not limited to moral arguments; this is a public health problem that is spiraling out of control.[23]

The CP80 Foundation's motto is to "Evolve the Internet to Protect Children." As found on CP80's website: "If a child looked at one pornography web page every 10 seconds he would be 538.775 years old when he finished looking at all the Internet Porn that exists today."[24]

NOTES

1. See R. Jenkins, "Violent Pornography Blamed for Turning Boy Aged 14 into a Rapist," *Times London*, 24 March 2006, as quoted in "The Porn Problems and Solutions," http://www.obscenitycrimes.org.
2. Reisman. "Psychopharmacology."
3. John L. Hart, "Fight to Stop Porn," *LDS Church News*, The Church of Jesus Christ of Latter-day Saints, 14 April 2007.
4. Available on http://www.thedeadkidsofmyspace.com.
5. R. Benson, "Will Glut of Online Porn Create More Young Sex Offenders?" *Citizen Magazine*, Nov. 2002, as quoted in "Harm to Children from Online Exposure to Hardcore Adult Pornography," htpp://www.obscenitycrimes.org, January 2010.
6. Carnes, *In the Shadows of the Net*, 12.
7. Ibid.
8. See Dr. David Delmonico, as quoted in The Lighted Candle Society Newsletter, June 2009.
9. Ibid.
10. See M. Conlon. "Web Skews Sex Education," *Reuters*, 16 May 2000, as quoted on "The Porn Problems and Solutions," http:// www.obscenitycrimes.org.
11. Dr. Victor B. Cline, "Pornography's Effects on Adults and Children," Morality in Media, 2001, as quoted on http://www.obscenitycrimes.org.
12. Available on http://www.thedeadkidsof myspace.com.
13. See Lt. Col. Dave Grossman, as quoted in Harmer and Smith, *The Sex Industrial Complex*, 91–93.
14. Ibid.
15. "Children's Interent Pornography Statistics," http://www.familysafemedia.com/pornography_statistics.html.
16. Kastleman, *The Drug of the New Millennium*, 4.
17. "Porn's New Customer," News Archives, 27 February 2008, http://www.cp80.org.
18. Ibid.

19. Kastleman, *The Drug of the New Millennium*, 7.
20. Available on http://www.thedeadkidsofmyspace.com. Name withheld.
21. Kastleman, *The Drug of the New Millennium*, 8.
22. See "Internet Addiction is Real," News Archives, 24 March 2008, The CP80 Foundation, http://www.cp80.org.
23. Ibid.
24. Ibid.

5

SOCIAL
NETWORKING

I myself must mix with action lest I wither by despair.

ALFRED, LORD TENNYSON

ave you ever had the unpleasant experience of telling a youth
that they can no longer go on their Facebook or MySpace
page? It's akin to telling them that you're going to cut off
their right arm. In many parents' experiences, the emotional
reaction is one you could expect to see in an addict facing with-
drawal. It should come as no surprise that both teen and adult
use of social networking sites has risen significantly. Statistics
show that "73% of wired American teens now use Social Networking websites, a significant increase from previous surveys.
Just over half of online teens (55%) used Social Networking sites
in November 2006, and 65% did so in February 2008."[1]

HOW YOUNG IS TOO YOUNG
FOR SOCIAL NETWORKING?

Facebook is one of the most popular social networking sites in
the world. You can bet that your children like it (some obsessively

and addictively so) and want to participate along with their peers. But are they old enough to be using it?

You can find kids who are as young as elementary school age on the sites. Some have accounts their parents don't know about. Some parents believe they can monitor and protect their kids on Facebook, while a lot of parents think social networking is harmless and have never seen their child's page. Most kids and parents are clueless about the dangers lurking on all social networking sites.

Facebook's terms of service clearly state, "You will not use Facebook if you are under 13." Facebook users are asked for their birthday when creating their account. The site uses this info to calculate age. Anyone under thirteen is turned away. The obvious trouble here is that kids also know how to calculate a birth year. So they just lie. Sometimes the consequences can be disastrous.

The specific concerns for parents should be their child's privacy, pedophiles, cyberbullying, and the ever-growing compulsive need to stay in frequent touch with their "friends" online.

For example, "49% of high school students have posted personal information on their web pages—such as name, age, or address—that could assist a stranger to identify or locate them."[2]

The "social" in social networking is the descriptive and key word here. Young kids aren't mature enough to be responsible on Facebook or other networks—they yak away about way too personal and identifying info (enough to be tracked down by predators), they can upload inappropriate photos, and they use inappropriate language with sexual content—and they don't understand that anything posted online is there forever.

Cyberbullying is also a serious problem on social networks. Cyberbullies can follow their victim home through the web. There are some privacy controls on social network sites that allow for some amount of control, but there are a lot of big, wide holes in those controls.

> ## Level 3 Sex Offender Met 15-Year-Old MySpace Friend
>
> MA—A Level 3 sex offender pushing 50 has been charged with enticement of a minor after police say he met a 15-year-old boy who had been corresponding with him on MySpace. Jones* 46, of Worcester, allegedly kissed the boy after meeting him at a local park. There, the two also reportedly took pictures of each other. The investigation oddly enough began after a clerk at a convenience store notified police that the suspect had been "hanging around" there and made her feel uncomfortable. Jones was earlier convicted of raping a child in 1988.[3]

KIDS SET UP SECRET ACCOUNTS UNBEKNOWNST TO PARENTS

Kids can set up other accounts created on friends' computers, with fake names that only their friends know about. No parent is omniscient (all knowing). Kids can create these other accounts and communicate in inappropriate or unsafe ways without a parent even knowing. That said, are parents going to have to give in at some point and let their child have a site at home that they can monitor?

At least refuse access until your children are thirteen—sixteen is more realistic and safer. They'll have some time to mature, and you'll have time to teach them how to be responsible and safe. Communicate and educate.

Sometimes they'll keep it a secret and do whatever they want anyway. So start communicating early. Set up your own Facebook site and search through your children's friends' sites. You just might find your child's picture on one of those sites under a fake name.

Take, for example, a thirteen-year-old girl whose mom discovered her MySpace account on their computer (which shows a lack of wise family Internet rules or just a rebellious young teen). After her mother made her shut down her MySpace account, the young teen pulled off a very well-prepared plan to establish another page. The thirteen-year-old waited for a teenage girls' church activity at another family's home and brought a very suggestive and older-looking photo of herself (lots of makeup with cheeks sucked in and eyes glancing upward). She waited for the right moment while the other girls were busy and having fun and spent some alone time in the family den with their scanner and Internet service, adding a new personal page under a sleazy, fake name, listing her age at sixteen.

Some of the abbreviations on her site are obvious and upsetting. The adults involved are clueless as to what some of her message means:

> **You R All: ***ked gann hoho xgirls 4:55dd3 Sprlocked@ loaded in a good way COMF MY C3WAY.**

Obviously, this thirteen-year-old was still too young and uninformed about the dangers of her post. She, unbelievably, even put her address on the page. Sadly, she meant it as an advertisement for boys but didn't realize that she had made herself an open invitation for a predator.

TN—A 31-year-old convicted sex offender has been arrested after police say he posed as a professional photographer on MySpace in order to meet and then sexually assault a 17-year-old girl, of Nashville. Smith* is accused of luring the alleged victim to a local motel after he convinced her to meet him there for a photo shoot. It was at the motel where the reported assault occurred. According to TV, he may have also assaulted another woman on February 1st, after luring her also through MySpace. On the profile he listed himself as age 27 and has even amassed over 600 friends. He has been charged with rape, false imprisonment, and four violations of the sex offender registry.[4]

LIMIT SOCIALIZING TO YOUR KNOWN FRIENDS

Even at seventeen, the girl in the above news report was a victim of not only a predator but also her own innocence. The obvious message here for social networking is *keep the socializing to your known friends.* Even at that, predators can still access your child's social life and information through your child's friends' pages (friends of friends).

According to Pew Internet statistics, surveys show that "today's teens face potential risks associated with online life," as follows:

- Some 32% of online teenagers (and 43% of social-networking teens) have been contacted online by complete strangers.

- 17% of online teens (31% of social networking teens) have "friends" on their social network profile who they have never personally met.[5]

Understand that your child can let anyone who requests to become their "friend" have access to their page and all their photos, personal profiles, and wall notes. (Some of their comments describe their schools, their hangouts, their activities, and so on.)

The more "friends" you have listed on your profile page, the more of an ego boost it is for most kids. Unless kids are educated and self-disciplined, some will agree to allow complete strangers onto their personal page. Data shows that "23% of teens who have been contacted by a stranger online say they felt scared or uncomfortable because of the online encounter."[6]

For predators (even though the youth may not communicate back and forth with this "friend" but has just added them to their "list of friends"), they now not only have access to the information by which they can track down your child's location, but they also can click onto the pages of your child's friends and have access to their information as well.

Of the above 43 percent of social-networking teens who have been contacted by strangers with "friend" requests, "21% of those teens have engaged an online stranger to find out more information about that person (that translates to 7% of all online teens).["7] Predators are notorious for posing as teenagers or friends with similar interests as your child to get their foot in the door, strike up a friendship, and begin to expertly "groom" the child as a friend they would like to meet up with or set up to humiliate online.

DEVELOPMENTALLY NEGATIVE EFFECTS OF SOCIAL NETWORKING

As reported by Dr. Jill Manning, predators aren't the only negative consequence of chatting networks. Patricia M. Greenfield, a researcher with the Children's Digital Media Center and the Department of Psychology at the University of California at Los Angeles, reviewed findings related to developmental effects and media. Greenfield paid close attention to chat rooms due to the popularity of this forum among youth. She concluded from her analysis of online communications in chat rooms that the following effects would likely occur for youth regularly involved in this mode of social interaction:[8]

1. Disinhibition in sexuality, aggression, and race relations [for example, making inappropriate comments about sexual activity or race that would be considered anti-social in other contexts or acting out sexually in risky, maladaptive, or illegal ways].

2. Early sexual priming.

3. Modeling of racism, negative attitudes toward women, and homophobia.

4. Breeding of personal and social irresponsibility due to anonymity.[9]

"We consider the Internet to be a repository of information," she further states, however, her "experience in the chat room led to the conclusion that we had better also think of the Internet in terms of the values that we wish to socialize."[10]

Exposure to information in cyberspace isn't just about your child introducing themselves to incredible amounts of positive information—it's also about the breeding ground of irresponsible, damaging, and sometimes dangerous behavior.

Man Posed as Teen on MySpace to Meet Girls, Three Victims Identified Thus Far

A 21-year-old man from Ohio has been indicted by a Grand Jury on charges that he posed as a 17-year-old on MySpace to meet underage girls. Harris (name changed), is accused of meeting at least three victims, 14, 15, and 16, in order to take pictures of the girls and have sex with at least two of them. He has been charged with four counts of illegal use of a minor in nudity-oriented material, two counts of unlawful sexual conduct with a minor, and one count of pandering sexually oriented material involving a minor.[11]

NOTES

1. Lenhart, "Social Media & Mobile Internet Use among Teens and Young Adults," http://www.pewinternet.org, accessed March 2010.
2. Kastleman, *The Drug of the New Millennium*, 7.
3. http://www.thedeadkidsofmyspace.com. Name changed.
4. Ibid. Name changed.
5. "Teens, Privacy and Online Social Networking/Summary of Findings," Pew Internet and American Life Project, 2007, accessed, March 2010, http://www.pewinternet.org. Bullets added.
6. Ibid.
7. Ibid.
8. See Jill C. Manning, MS, Testimony. "Submission for the Record." *Hearing on Pornography's Impact on Marriage & the Family,* subcommittee on the Constitution, Civil Rights and Property Rights, committee on Judiciary, United States Senate, November 10, 2005.
9. Ibid.
10. Ibid.
11. http://www.thedeadkidsofmyspace.com.

6

A NEW FOREIGN LANGUAGE
TO PARENTS

?4 U. R U <:-1 about this lingo your youth uses in their world of cyberspace and mobile devices? Some of the following abbreviations may be familiar to you, some you can figure out yourself, but there's also a world of cyberspace and mobile-device idioms that the average adult can't decipher. A lot of the abbreviations are meant to be secretive.

DNT B CYEO. DNT B >:-11. DNT B 7K. U R NOT AN IWIAM—just educate yourself! If your youth is texting or instant messaging (even if you check up on them), the chat lingo can throw what's akin to a foreign language into the mix that parents or guardians can't translate and you've got a wider generation gap, and a form of communication that is senseless to those responsible for our youth.

We've experienced the materialization of a new language which is not only designed to be compacted to facilitate the speed of their communication but also geared to different online interests. This new coded jargon gives our youth (and also predators) the freedom to communicate both openly and secretly at the same time.

Statistics show that "95% of parents didn't recognize common chat room lingo that teenagers use to let people they're chatting with know that their parents are watching,"[1] such as, POS (parent over shoulder). It's not only used in chat rooms but kids (and adults) can also use this abbreviated language when texting.

JTLYK, they're **KPC**!

The first table below is the "Top 20 Codes and Acronyms" provided by spectorsoft.com:[2]

TEXT AND CHAT ABBREVIATION DICTIONARY

8 Oral sex	**AEAP** As early as possible
1337 Elite *or* leet	**ALAP** As late as possible
143 I love you	**ASL** Age/Sex/Location
182 I hate you	**CD9, Code 9** Parents are around
1174 Nude club	**C-P** Sleepy
420 Marijuana	**F2F** Face-to-face
459 I love you	**GNOC** Get naked on cam
ADR Address	**GYPO** Get your pants off

HAK
Hugs and kisses

IWSN
I want sex now

ILU
I love you

J/O
Jerking off

Below is a top fifty pick. Some chat lingo is often offensive, and you might not be aware that your youth would even communicate like this. For more abbreviation dictionaries, use an Internet search engine.

7K
Sick

A3
Anytime, anywhere, anyplace

20
Location

ASL, A/S/L, ASLA
Age, Sex, Location

121
Private chat initiation

BRB, BBS
Be right back, Be back soon

404
I don't know

B4N
Bye for now

420
Let's get high, *or* marijuana

BCNU
Be seeing you

555
Sobbing, crying

BT
Bite this

88
Hugs and kisses

CYA
Cover your a** *or*
See Ya

CYEO
Crying your eyes out

DBEYR
Don't believe every-
thing you read

DILLIGAS
Do I look like I give a
sh**

E
Ecstasy

DUM
Do you masturbate?

ILUVUM
I love you, man

JTLYK
Just to let you know

KIT
Keep in touch

KPC
Keeping parents
clueless

FUD
Fear, uncertainty, and
disinformation

IWIAM
Idiot within a moron

ILY
I love you

IRL:-x
I'm keeping my mouth
shut

>:-11
Mad, angry

<3, </3, <33333333
Love or friendship
Broken Heart
Lots of love

IRL
In real life

ISO
In search of

J/K
Just kidding

L8R
Later

LMAO
Laughing my a** off

LOL
Laughing out loud *or*
Lots of Love

LYLAS
Love you like a sister

NP
No problem *or*
Nosy parents

NUB
New person to a site
or game

OT
Off topic

PAW, POS, (CD9, 911)
Parents are around,
Parent over shoulder
Parent is watching

RT
Real time

SH
Sh** happens

SorG
Straight or Gay?

STBY
Sucks to be you

SWAK
Sealed (or sent) with
a kiss

TTYL
Talk to you later *or*
type to you later

TYVM
Thank you very much

WEG
Wicked evil grin

WTF
What the f***

WYWH
Wish you were here

NOTES

1. Kastleman, *The Drug of the New Millennium*, 8.
2. "Internet Lingo Dictionary, Top 20 Codes and Acronyms," available on http://www.spectorsoft.com.

7

WEBCAMS

If you have children and you do not need to have a webcam, do not have one on your computer.

BSECURE.COM

THE DANGERS OF USING WEBCAMS

Do you want your children's bedroom to become a window through which the entire cyberworld can view their personal lives? As described so well by Bsecure Online:

> Kids these days are accustomed to sharing their lives with the world on blogs and social networking sites like MySpace. And now, through the use of webcams, kids are able to give the world a window right into their bedrooms. This creates a whole new level of risk that parents and educators must be able to protect children from.
>
> Webcams are video cameras, usually attached directly to a computer, that send images to the World Wide Web. These images can be still photos, a series of images sent in succession, or streaming video.
>
> Webcams are small, cheap, and easy to use, making them accessible to kids and teenagers. In most cases, all you have to do to set one up is plug it into a computer and install the software. You

can then use it to videoconference with other webcam owners, or you can post a link to your webcam on one of the many webcam sites on the Internet. *Anybody who visits that site can then view the images from your webcam.*[1]

HACKERS CAN ACTIVATE A WEBCAM WITHOUT THE USER'S KNOWLEDGE

Do you think your child can be trusted with a webcam? No doubt in your mind that they're obeying your rules? All right, assume that your child is obeying your webcam rules or attempting to be discreet with its use—here's a sobering thought for you:

> There are some webcams that automatically post the URL of the webcam on a website when the software is installed. Even users who do not post their webcams on one of these sites could find their lives being shared with the world. Each webcam has a web address that can be found by search engines, who will then post it among their listings.
>
> Usually each camera has a password that must be used to access the webcam, but many users do not bother to change the default password that their webcams came with. There are also Trojan horse programs that allow hackers to activate a webcam without the user's knowledge.[2]

PROWLING PEDOPHILES CAN HACK INTO WEBCAMS

Let's throw an additional threat into the mix. Pedophiles can prowl around in cyberspace search engines, find your family's (or your child's) web address, and then hack into it and activate the webcam without the knowledge of anyone in the household. "That webcam now poses a serious risk to children because it has provided a visual link with online predators."[3]

Predators also scan webcam sites to find children and teenagers with webcams and then try to convince the children to expose themselves or do things on camera in exchange for money and gifts.[4]

This process usually happens gradually, with the predators starting with innocent-seeming requests and then asking the child to go one step further each time. In some cases, children have gone to the extent of setting up their own self-published pornography web sites, with subscription services available to anybody who wants to watch them.[5]

SAFE WEBCAM USE

We know that webcams can have many valuable uses, such as business use from your home, up-close visits with relatives and friends, and so on. And they can also be a handy tool for parents to check up on their kids at home while they're away.

"Safe webcam use" as stated by Bsecure.com, "simply requires taking certain precautions to make sure that access to them is restricted to only certain people." These protective measures include:

- If you have children and you do not need to have a webcam, do not have one on your computer.

- If you have a computer with a webcam, keep it in a common room, not in a child's bedroom.

- Teach your children to use webcams only to communicate with people they know.

- When you are not using your webcam, put the lens cap on or unplug it.

- Make sure children understand that what they do on a webcam is not necessarily private. Teach them to never do anything in front of a webcam that they wouldn't want the entire world to see.

- Don't post your webcam URL on the web.

- Teach children about the dangers of posting personal information and pictures online.

- Teach children to not respond to instant messages or emails from strangers.[6]

WEBCAMS ARE ONLY THE LEADING EDGE

From *In the Shadows of the Net*, we find these sobering thoughts: "Today's streaming and Webcam technology were developed predominately by the pornography industry because it recognized the enormous potential for profit. That profit potential is always there, waiting for the next innovation."[7]

This is why we believe we are seeing only the leading edge of the cyberspace and sex addiction problem. It is imperative for society to acknowledge this situation. It would be fruitless, though certainly tempting, to simply stick our collective head in the sand and pretend nothing like this will happen or to roll our eyes and write off the issue as a fringe problem among a few "perverts."[8]

NOTES

1. "The Dangers of Using Webcams," Bsmart Articles, http://www.bsecure .com, "Ultimate Family Protection," italics added.
2. Ibid.
3. Ibid.
4. See ibid.
5. Ibid.
6. Ibid.
7. Carnes, *In the Shadows of the Net*, 214–15.
8. Ibid., 215.

SECTION III

THE RISKS OF
MOBILE DEVICES

8

CELL PHONES AND
ELECTRONIC GADGETS

*The good Lord set definite limits on man's wisdom, but set
no limits on his stupidity.*

KONRAD ADENAUER

ew Internet statistics show that cell phone ownership is nearly
ubiquitous [everywhere] among teens and young adults. Furthermore, much of the growth in teen cell phone ownership has
been driven by adoption among the youngest teens.[1]

THERE IS NO SUBSTITUTE FOR
PARENTAL SUPERVISION

If your child is under sixteen, why do they even need a cell
phone? Does having a mobile device guarantee that you can always
have a way to get in touch with your child? Of course not. They
can always claim that the reason for not staying in touch was that
their reception wasn't good or that their phone battery had run out
of charge.

The first and most important thing for any parent or guardian to
remember is that there is *no* substitute for parental communication

and supervision. The average parent is not going to prohibit their child from having a cell phone, hence the vital need to communicate with him and set down rules about cell phone use.

CELL PHONE SAFETY

Your role is to help your children use cell phones safely. First, talk with them about their phone use and set some solid ground rules. Second, explain your concerns and reasons, and monitor their text and picture messages. The trouble with parental monitoring of texts and picture messaging is that youth can delete messages and pictures before they even get home.

> New York: A young man, 26, was taken into custody after police say he collected cell phone numbers from young teen girls on MySpace and Facebook and sent sexual related text messages and pictures to their cell phones. Authorities say he also offered his apartment located in Jamestown to anyone who felt like running away from home.[2]

Even though parental rules, supervision, and communication are the first line of defense, we do recommend researching parental control options that may be available through your cell phone provider.

Programs are available, such as "My Mobile Watchdog," that allow parents and guardians to monitor calls from and to the cell phone as well as text messages, emails, and picture messages. It immediately alerts you if he or she receives unapproved email, text messages, or phone calls. You will receive parental alerts and can see an actual copy of:

- Text Messages (SMS) sent and received along with their full content.

- Photos (MMS) sent and received with text messages (on select phones).

- Emails sent and received along with their full content.

- Logs of calls made and received including time and duration.[3]

In the past five years, cell phone ownership has become mainstream among even the youngest teens, with fully "71% of 12- to 17-year-olds now owning a cell phone in early 2008,"[4] "up from just 18% as recently as 2004,"[5] with "85% of adults now having a cell phone."[6]

Cell phone ownership by our youth is not just a passing fad. It's not just a craze that's going to die down and fade away. It's a technology that's ever growing and obsessively used by the majority of our youth already. If not closely regulated by parents, it's going to be irresponsibly used by impulsive youth who, if left to their own devices, can make dangerous choices with cell phone communication and put themselves at risk. The danger of cell phone connection to the Internet can lead to activities that are going to bring with it some serious consequences for some of our youth and contribute to an already decaying morality in society.

TEXT MESSAGING

Are parents aware that text messaging by teens now surpasses face-to-face contact? Or of the alarming rate of how rapidly daily text messaging among American teens has shot up in the past eighteen months? For example, "38 percent of teens texted friends daily in February of 2008, to *54 percent of teens texting daily in September 2009*. Teens are sending enormous quantities of text messages a day:"[7]

- Half of teens send 50 or more text messages a day, or 1,500 texts a month.

- One in three send more than 100 texts a day, or more than 3,000 texts a month.

- The youngest teen boys are the most resistant to texting—averaging 20 messages per day.[8]

The results of a study on teens and their cell phones by Amanda Lenhart, a senior researcher at the Pew Internet and American Life Project, absolutely cements the message of this entire chapter. Lenhart "surveyed 800 pairs of teens and parents, and organized focus groups with children in four different cities. During the focus groups, she says she was amazed to discover the teens were secretly texting under the tables as they talked with researchers."[9]

> When researchers asked if teens ever turned their phones off, the majority looked at the interviewers in "horror," says Lenhart. The kids said they might put their phone on silent or vibrate—but off? Highly unlikely.
>
> They would never actually want to cut themselves off from that network of communication that the phone represented, . . . the teens even slept with their phones. Many said they kept the phone under their pillow so it was quieter during the night. But others said they kept it under the pillow so they would hear or feel it, and be able to answer or text in the middle of the night.[10]

CYBERBULLYING

There is an ever-growing incidence of cyberbullying (researchers say that 42 percent of kids have been bullied while online), which sometimes even leads to violence and suicide. According to new research, cyberbullying is now becoming more serious than conventional bullying.

About 10 percent of high school students are victims of bullying from cyberspace. Unlike the neighborhood or school bully, cyberbullies don't give their victims a break from their continuous harassment. Since bullying has now graduated into the limitless boundaries of cyberspace, the problem can be even more serious than conventional bullying.

IT'S NOT ABOUT TRUST, IT'S ABOUT MATURITY AND SAFETY

The first thing you should do after reading this is go access your youths' cell messages. Remember this: you brought them into this world, you pay for their room and board, you pay for the mortgage or rent on the house, and you buy their food and clothes. You're responsible for their emotional and physical health and safety—legally and morally.

Children of all ages should be allowed a certain amount of personal privacy, but when it comes to their safety and health, you have every right to access a record of their free time and the quality of their texting.

A surprise visit to their cell phone history shouldn't raise up too much dust if there's been no risky behavior occurring. Some of their texting or social networking is filled with foreign-looking jargon that you'll need to write down and look up in a chat abbreviation dictionary. A lot of their communications are worthless chatter (at least to an adult): "Love you, Babe. Miss you, Babe. Are you still grounded? That's so unfair! He's so cool! Meet me here—meet me there." It should be nothing they couldn't say in person—unless, of course, you find they're cyberbullying, being cyberbullied, or it contains sexual content (or images); illegal drug discussion; info on participating in activities they shouldn't; and so on. There are dialogue and photos that you hope you'll never find on their phone. You might get a lot of static if you try to look—so be prepared and be firm.

ACCESSING YOUR CHILD'S TEXT MESSAGES

You can find use instructions on your child's cell phone on the provider's website by looking up the model number of the phone and printing a user guide from the website (remember, you can Google *anything*). Select your phone brand and then the model. A window will pop up with an interactive user guide to teach you how to use the features of the phone.

A cellular telephone is sometimes a good way to ensure you can get in touch with your older child. (If you feel the need for your younger child to carry a cell phone, purchase a call only phone.)

Keep in mind that even if a cell phone with a screen doesn't have Internet access, pornography can still be accessed from flash cards (also known as SIM cards). Flash cards are small plastic cards that fit into mobile devices and cameras and attach to computers with a special USB attachment. Flash cards can have pornography downloaded onto them and then pornographic material brought inside the home (or the school or library) without a person ever accessing the Internet from home. Most flash cards are interchangeable between a handheld device and a computer.

> New Mexico: John Smith (name changed) of Las Cruces has been charged with 12 counts of sexual exploitation of a child after he allegedly met two young girls, 13 and 14, over a popular social networking website. Several nude images of the victims were identified on his cell phone.[11]

Remember, a cell phone has both benefits and risks. The risks can sometimes be deadly. It is important for every parent or guardian to consider a child's age and the risks and benefits before purchasing a phone and to take an active role in helping his or her child learn to use cell phones safely.

A LETTER FOR THE PROTECTION
OF CHILDREN AND FAMILIES

The following, a letter from the Religious Alliance Against Pornography and the National Coalition for the Protection of Children and Families, is a strongly worded warning letter sent to congregations across the United States.

Reacting to perilous times, a wide range of religious leaders have united to sign one of the most forthright anti-pornography letters to date.

> In direct communication with many of the largest wireless companies, we have learned that they do not intend to warn parents at the time of purchase about the dangers of Internet pornography.
>
> This means that the educational process with parents to protect their children by not buying access to the Internet until adequate safety devices are in place must be done by the faith community now.
>
> We, the members of the Religious Alliance Against Pornography and the National Coalition for the Protection of Children & Families, wish to share with you a disturbing reality now affecting the most innocent and vulnerable among us: America's children and youth.
>
> Pornography and other sexually explicit material are now readily available on any wireless mobile device with Internet capabilities. Our children and grandchildren are at risk as well as those children entrusted to our spiritual leadership and care. Entire families, thus whole communities, stand to become victims of the immeasurable moral, social and spiritual damage which results.
>
> Most disconcerting is the fact that children's entertainment devices have become venues for explicit sexual content. Today's technologies facilitate the distribution of digital video content

as never before. Wireless handheld devices such as video cell phones, iPods, iPhones, PDAs, and PlayStations and other video game consoles are now conduits for all the pornography available on the Internet. Pornography has gone from between the mattresses to the cinema screen, to the television screen, to the computer screen and now to the wireless screen. Handheld pornography is no longer a futuristic threat.

Parents cannot and must not expect government and the wireless industry alone to protect their children from the harms of the wireless culture. Until recently no filtering devices for wireless technology were available. The five largest wireless companies, T-Mobile, AT&T, Sprint Nextel, Alltel, and Verizon are seriously committed to developing filtering technology. But to date, only T-Mobile, AT&T and Alltel have made publicly available such an Internet blocking tool.

Let's be very clear. Wireless technology is not the enemy. Rather, the danger lies in the perverse misuse of the technology and the fact that safeguards are limited in both availability and reliability. Exposure to unwanted, seductive and explicit content downloadable from the Internet onto these wireless handheld devices is a real and present danger. Further, children and teens are vulnerable to sexual predators who readily approach them through the Internet.[12]

"The letter encourages leaders of congregations and parents to keep people informed of 'real time accurate information' of inherent dangers. The letter further warns that every child in America will be impacted directly or indirectly."[13]

MOBILE GADGETS

You must be realistic and realize that:

Pornographers are continually on the offensive and are determined to seduce those not seeking pornography and force their depravity on us. They have learned how to manipulate innocent people from good sites to pornographic sites. Every child will have some peers or friends of peers that are plugged into the Internet through a wireless device. As stated in the above letter, **wireless handheld devices such as video cell phones, iPods, iPhones,**

PDAs, and Playstations and other video game consoles are *now* *conduits for all the pornography available on the Internet.*[14]

Pew Internet tells us that "among teens, the average person owns 3.5 gadgets out of five: cell phones, MP3 players, computers, game consoles and portable gaming devices."[15]

Let's take a closer look at the mobile "gadgets" the average teen owns. Many parents give these high-tech gifts (including cell phones) to their kids without even knowing the capabilities or the dangers of the device that can get their kids in trouble.

iTunes: A free application for a Mac or PC. It organizes and plays your digital music and video off a computer. It syncs all your media with your iPod, iPhone, and Apple TV. And it's a store on your computer, iPod touch, iPhone, or Apple TV that has everything you need to be entertained. Anywhere. Anytime.

MP3 Player: A digital audio player, or DAP. It is an electronic device that has the primary function of storing, organizing, and playing audio files. Content is placed on the device by connecting it to a computer, typically via a USB. Originally, when purchased, the device comes with special software on a CD-Rom or you go to the manufacturer's website and download the software onto your computer. That will then allow you to download your favorite songs. These devices are getting more and more advanced with screens and "libraries" that can allow the downloading of not only tunes but also other content such as TV episodes or movies. They are also referred to as portable media players with image-viewing and/or video-playing support.

iPod: A portable media player that can have tunes, photos, videos, games, contact information, email settings, web bookmarks, and calendars (depending on the mode) transferred to it. At a touch, users can access all kinds of media that includes explicit songs and mature movies and TV shows, and kids can also surf the web.

BlackBerry: A handheld wireless device that can read out your email and calendars; most models also function as cell phones. BlackBerries come with complete alphanumeric keyboards.

Bluetooth: An open, wireless technology device for exchanging data over short distances (using short length radio waves) from fixed and mobile devices. Bluetooth provides a secure way to connect and exchange information between devices such as faxes, mobile phones, telephones, laptops, personal computers, printers, Global Positioning System (GPS) receivers, digital cameras, and video game consoles. A "master" can hook up with as many as seven "slaves" to share data. The master and slaves can then all swap whatever "spit" they want to share back and forth. (In some cases "spit" is putting it mildly.)

HidePod: Allows the owner to hide information behind a calculator on an iPod or an iPhone. The calculator appears by default on the touch and iPhone. To open HidePod, you enter a code using the calculator controls. Then, the hidden media files open and you can browse the secret collection of programs and media files that have been hidden. HidePod is designed to be stealthy and covert, so it might not be easy to find. You can try to discover the pass code that opens it. It is a string of numbers enclosed in decimal points. To open the calculator, enter ".8008." and see if HidePod opens. This number, .8008., is the default code. Or sometimes a youth will use their birth date or some other set of numbers (your address number, for example). Don't forget the decimal points at the beginning and end of the number. If you don't enter the pass code, Hide-Pod will just function like the calculator.

What do you do if you can't find your way into hidden files? Presumably the youth is going to deny it's there or he wouldn't have hidden it in the first place. You need to look at the serial number of the phone. If you can't find it on the phone or in the battery compartment, you can always find it by opening "Settings" on the phone, choosing "General," and selecting "About." The serial number will be listed. Enter the serial number on HidePod's site on the Internet. If a registration number is returned, your youth is hiding something.

CELL PHONE TECHNOLOGY IS CONSTANTLY ADVANCING

Be aware that the technology and availability of mobile devices is continually changing, and parents always need to educate themselves (Google!) on any device their child wants to own (or borrow). One of the latest cell phones has the ability to instant message (IM) with live streaming video between both parties at the same time as they communicate with each other.

NOTES

1. See Lenhart, "Social Media & Mobile Internet Use Among Teens and Young Adults," http://www.pewinternet.org. Accessed March 2010.
2. Available on http://thedeadkidsofmyspace.com.
3. "Stop Cyber-Bullying on Your Child's Cell Phone!" Available on http://www.mymobilewatchdog.com, a registered trademark of eAgency Inc., 2009.
4. Amanda Lenhart, Rich Ling, Kristen Purcell, and Kathryn Zickuhr. "Teens and Mobile Phones," Pew Internet, accessed Dec. 2010, http://www.pewinternet.org.
5. Lenhart, "Social Media & Mobile Internet Use among Teens and Young Adults," http://www.pewinternet.org.
6. Amanda Lenhart. "Adults and Cell Phones," Pew Internet, http://www.pewinternet.org. Accessed December 2010.
7. Lenhart, "Teens and Mobile Phones," http://www.pewinternet.org. Italics added.
8. Ibid. Bullets added.
9. Patti Neighmond, "Working to Stop Teens Texting Behind the Wheel," NPR's Morning Edition, May 10, 2010, as quoted on Pew Internet, http://www.pewinternet.org. Accessed May 2010.
10. Ibid.
11. Available on http://www.thedeadkidsofmyspace.com.

12. See "Internet Wide Open for Children's Games," *LDS Church News*, The Church of Jesus Christ of Latter-day Saints, Saturday, Nov. 17, 2007.
13. Ibid.
14. Ibid. Bold added.
15. See Pew Internet, http://www.pewinternet.org.

9

SEXTING

What the eye doesn't see the heart doesn't grieve over.

AMERICAN PROVERB

Sexting is really a combination of two words, *sexy* and *texting*. Remember the advice given in chapter 5 on cell phones? The risks of having cell phone capability to share photos at the touch of a button is sometimes too much for youth to resist. In the blink of an eye, the send button can be pushed. Once a photo leaves the phone, there is no way of retrieving it. It can't be taken back, and the sender has no control whatsoever over where it goes next or how many people will end up seeing it—now or in the future.

WHY DO KIDS SEXT?

Do you know for sure that your children aren't sending nude pictures to friends? Not a pleasant thought, but a quick picture of yourself taken privately sometimes just doesn't feel like an invasion of one's modesty. Sometimes modesty isn't even an issue; kids are sending sexually explicit photos of their private body parts or videos of actual sex acts to those they want to hook up with, simply to impress others.

IT'S ILLEGAL!

Sexting is illegal. It is currently a felony for children under age eighteen to send or be in possession of such messages. It is considered distribution of child pornography, and violators can be charged and end up on the sex offender registry. (Some states have lowered the offense from a felony to a misdemeanor for someone younger than eighteen.)

Kids have been showing off to each other since the beginning of time. Girls have been trying to impress guys, and guys have been strutting their stuff—not only to the opposite sex but also to their peers. When pressure comes from a boyfriend or girlfriend, or friends, it's easy enough for them to lack foresight in what they send. History shows that kids who show off can be very irresponsible; now, with new technologies, there's much more harm that can be done than ever before.

Kids are going to say that they trust the recipient(s) and naïvely assume that their pictures will not be shared with others. Here's where the lack of foresight comes in. What if a relationship ends? What happens if the receiver loses his or her phone, or a friend gets access to it? The issue of trust is extremely inconsistent in the world of preteens and teens. Some youth can also be thoughtless and mean-spirited. Sexting has even led to suicide by kids who were bullied over public exposure of their sexted photo.

COMMUNICATE AND EDUCATE

It's time to open that dialogue with your youth—in addition to having them share the photos on their cell phone and social networks with you. Whether or not you discover any sexting, it's imperative that you make sure your child doesn't have (or continue to have) a phone with a camera. Most important of all, discuss sexting with your children.

"PORNDEMIC ALERT: KIDS TRADING PICS."

From the CP80 Foundation we read: "I've seen everything from your basic striptease to sexual acts being performed," police Detective Brian Marvin, a member of the FBI Cyber Crime Task Force of Central Ohio told Fox News. "You name it, they will do it at their home under this perceived anonymity."[1] He wasn't talking about adults. Detective Marvin was talking about the growing trend in teen dating: sharing homemade pornographic pictures and videos.

Teens record themselves engaged in sex acts with their cell phone or webcam. Many girls think they need to do it to catch a boy's attention. "A lot more girls are aggressive," explained one 18-year-old senior. "Some girls are crazy and they are putting themselves out there." Children are growing up in a world awash in pornographic images. They are not emotionally mature enough to process these images, and distinguish between what is real, and what is not.

Jean Twenge, a psychology professor at San Diego State says kids just don't get it. "Adolescents are not known for thinking things through—that's a generational constant," she said. [Teens] don't see it that way.[2]

NOTES

1. See "Porndemic Alert: Kids Trading Pics," http://www.cp80.org, News Archive, created April 15, 2008.
2. Ibid.

SECTION IV

INCREASING AND TRANSFORMING YOUR COMMUNICATION

WITH YOUR CHILDREN

10

GAMING

Tell me what amusements you like best and whether
your amusements have become a ruling passion
in your life, and I will tell you what you are.

JOSEPH F. SMITH

"KIDDIE CRACK"

It may interest you to know that video games have been compared to "kiddie crack." As you will read below, these virtual, competitive games can suck your youth into a world of compulsion (and sometimes violence) that can take away from the quality of their lives.

If it's a problem in your child's life, this chapter can help you fix that (or prevent gaming from becoming a problem). One of the secrets to intelligent and effective parenting in this particular area of cyberspace technology is to successfully manage what, when, and how your children play. Excessive time spent on the Internet can be addictive as it is, let alone adding the competitive, compulsive, and sometimes violent nature of game playing to the mix. Children who play four to five hours per day have no time for socializing, doing homework, or playing sports. (Childhood obesity is also increasing among gamers.) All of the above certainly takes away from normal social development.

There is such a thing as a healthy and fun relationship with video gaming, but keep in mind that it does have to involve effective education (both for you and for your child) and management of game playing. A heavy-handed ban on game playing in many cases isn't going to influence your child's behavior in a positive manner and can be damaging to your relationship.

THE EFFECTS OF VIOLENT GAMING SHOWS ON BRAIN MRI'S

Some kids play horrifically violent and sexual games, and you need to know the exact content of their games. If gaming has become the "enemy" in your home, then read on—educate yourself and then begin working with your child.

Consider this vital information from Dr. W. Dean Belnap, specialist in pediatrics and child/adolescent psychiatry.

"Many of the problems with teens today," Dr. Belnap explains to us, "can be traced to violent video games, television programs, and movies. Students act out the scenes on their screens because reality has become what they take in day after day. That reality is violence."[1]

It should be of concern to all parents and society in general that MRI brain scans show changes in the functioning of a preteen or teen's brain when they play violent video games. As you will read below from Dr. Belnap, this current scientific data on the loss of brain function relating to gaming is significant and profoundly informative.

Teens that play violent video games show definite changes in MRI brain scans. Using functional Magnetic Resonance Imagery, adolescents who were playing video games showed loss of prefrontal lobe function. The amygdala stimulated the basal ganglia to take control as the imprinting of brain cells called for increased anger, tension, and trauma.

Oddly enough, the trauma is just beginning because the loss of brain power will be manifest in more than just MRI scans. A teenager addicted to violent video games or other violent media risks a greater likelihood of violent behavior and further addictions beyond just screenplay.

Why? Because the ability to reason, think, judge, and calculate has been diminished. They are not developing self-discipline; they are not learning to be charitable to others; they are not studying, playing outside, or talking to anyone. Even their cell phones and instant messages may take a secondary position when the video games are in control.

Parents complain about the hours wasted playing video games. But time is not all that is wasted. Brain scan comparisons of those who obsess with video games and those who don't, show graphically that the group of non-playing teens exhibited more activation in the frontal cortex. In other words, the dendrites were multiplying and the brain was functioning at a higher level.

The group fixated with violence showed diminished function in the prefrontal cortex and increased activity in the right amygdala as well as activation in the right basal ganglia more than the left. In other words, they had slipped into more animal-like instincts.[2]

Below is an actual listing of the "content" of one of the games for purchase in an Internet online gaming catalog:

"Rated Mature—17+. Content: Intense violence, blood, language, partial nudity, sexual violence and content. In amazing 3-D. Add to Cart: $39.95. Free Demo."

It could have been much worse; it could have been nudity, which is, of course, full nudity as opposed to "partial" nudity. However, the intense violence is probably vivid dismemberment, and the sexual violence is rape in virtual reality. Those are the objectives of the game and the achievements that give you the thrill of progressing to a higher level.

The above content description from an online catalog, which offered a smorgasbord of downloadable game genres to select from, had only a menacing-looking soldier on the cover and was in a war genre. It didn't look too bad until you read the content.

MULTIPLAYER GAMES

Gaming is even more challenging when you go online and hook into multiplayer games. Multiplayer games—where millions of people are playing at once, twenty-four hours a day—are only played online. The gamer can choose his "fantasy" game, his role, and his conquest. Gamers can also communicate with each other as they play.

The social aspect of multiplayer gaming is also an attraction to some youth. Kids can join and play in groups, or they can join permanent groups called "clans." The clans usually schedule times and days for everyone to meet and play. These clans, with their pressure to succeed, can also open up the door for cyberbullying.

Online gaming sites are also the playground of predators. Current studies show that child predators are using the features within gaming consoles to start online friendships with youth and begin the grooming process to lure kids into meeting in person.

CHOOSE YOUR FANTASY

Try initiating a web search (Google, Yahoo, and so on) and type in "PC game downloads," or "Mac games," or "online games." When a gaming catalog site opens, note how some of them contain links to "online chat rooms." One online gaming catalog site in particular greets the Internet user with the deep, sexy, alluring voice of "Amber" offering the opportunity to order a live chat to "get to know her better." (Remember, youth should not be allowed into chat rooms. Use either parental controls or a software filter program to disable the feature—and these aren't always foolproof.)

There are games offered from all kinds of genres: role playing, action, babes, and so on. One game in the "babes" genre had a cartoon woman on the cover, very scantily clad, with large, exaggerated breasts, small waist, overly shapely hips, and she was in bondage with her hands tied above her head. The most disturbing detail of all was the smile on her face. Perhaps this particular genre doesn't offend some males as much as it does females. Young women are often the exploited victims of the violent sexual conquest provided to young people (mostly males) in gaming.

Is this what you want your teenager playing, sometimes compulsively for hours on end? In extreme cases, where a particularly hot game is going, some males stay at their computers for hours and hours. They are so obsessed that they won't leave to get up to eat, to sleep, or even to go to the bathroom. Some spend up to fifty to sixty hours a week. Time can simply slip away for gamers (and if grown-ups care about *limiting their own brain function,* there are time restrictions they can place upon themselves). Gaming software for both content and time restrictions is available for you to utilize. In the very extreme cases mentioned above, parents need to seek medical treatment at an addiction center for their child.

Obviously, as evidenced by the popularity and success of violent video games, violence does sell. It is clearly up to parents to do a better job of reducing the exposure of media violence to youth.

Many parents don't know exactly what the game content includes and don't see a need to screen these materials from their children. Therefore, the process begins with educating yourself. Ask your youth to show you the games they play, or look at the browser history of what gaming sites they've been on or see games they've downloaded. What your child fills his time with and compulsively plays in your home is your business and your responsibility.

EXPOSURE TO MATURE CONTENT

A survey conducted by Pew Internet and the American Life Project (supported by the John D. and Catherine T. MacArthur Foundation) was the first national survey of its kind. It found that "virtually all American teens play computer, console, or cell phone games."[3]

Another major finding is that game playing sometimes involves exposure to mature content, "with almost a third of teens playing games that are listed as appropriate only for people older than they are."[4]

There are some online games such *Diablo II*, *The Dark Age of Camelot*, *Grand Theft Auto*, *World of Warcraft*, and so on, that can pose complex problems for youth (and adults). Take the game *Diablo II*, for instance. It has incredible replay value, and most important, it blatantly advertises itself as offering a lot of "addictive" game play in either the single-player or the multiplayer mode (gamers call it "Heroin II"). *Diablo II* is a dark, fantasy-themed action/role-playing game, with elements of the hack and slash and "dungeon roaming" genres.

The constant Internet chat that goes on between gamers during these intense games and the extreme competitive nature of fighting with or against other gamers can make it hard to get up and take a break from the game or even quit when you need to.

Although some parents are becoming more concerned about their youth's online gaming obsessions, even some therapists and counselors don't understand how compulsive and addictive these games can become. When a parent tells a youth to just simply "turn off the computer," it can be akin to telling a smoker to "just stop smoking" or an alcoholic to "just quit drinking."

Unfortunately, it is sometimes impossible to try to limit a gamer's playing—the game has become the only thing that matters to the player. Sometimes parents are stuck, and no one takes them seriously or believes that a real problem exists. If you are in such a situation where your child (or an adult in your home) is showing signs of gaming addiction—plays almost every day, plays for more than four hours at a time, sacrifices social life for gaming, or grows ill-tempered or irritated if he can't play—then make some phone calls to addiction programs in your area. They will be able to tell you the proper therapist to contact. Or you can find an Internet addiction treatment specialist through an Internet search.

An interesting side note is that a large percentage of kids, when restricted to nonviolent/nonsexual games, enjoyed them as much as they did the mature content games. However, even though youth may be playing acceptable games, excessive gaming is a problem. Remember, if your youth is having trouble restricting his time at gaming—if it's affecting his homework time, friend time, or sleep, and he's agitated and non-cooperative about limiting gaming—you need to seek treatment for him. Addictive gaming could also be a symptom of depression or an attempt to escape from the real world.

Take note, "In immersion virtual reality, your brain experiences the fantasies as reality . . . with virtual reality, logic takes a back seat to sensual perception."[5]

THE ENTERTAINMENT SOFTWARE RATING BOARD (ESRB)

All parents need a game rating board that can fully alert them to the content of games played by their youth. The Entertainment Software Rating Board (ESRB) is a non-profit, self-regulatory body established in 1994. The ESRB is an invaluable, informative tool for parents of children of all ages. The ESRB assigns computer and video game content ratings, enforces industry-adopted advertising guidelines, and helps ensure responsible online privacy practices for the interactive entertainment software industry. To enter ESRB's website, go to www.ESRB.org and simply type the name of the game in question into the search block provided.

THE NATURE OF THE KILLING FIELD HAS CHANGED

Do you remember when we as "a nation watched as students went to school hefting guns and ammo rather than books in backpacks and picked off victims in video game style? With each kill, they cackled and shouted and in the end shot themselves as well"?[6] Dr. Belnap enlightens us further:

> A major source of entertainment for millions is making large numbers of people die on screen. While games used to invite slaughter of gangsters or aliens, today some "games" capitalize on blowing away ordinary people who have done nothing wrong—pedestrians, marching bands, elderly folk. And the saga continues. At some point, the nature of the killing field is no longer animated nor a dress rehearsal. Young people are being invited to enjoy the killing of others. How can a sniper randomly pick off unsuspecting citizens at a gas pump? Because the lines have blurred between real and not real. It has happened across the country. It will happen again and again because of negative imprints on the brain.[7]

NOTES

1. Belnap, *A Brain Gone Wrong*, 76.
2. Ibid., 76–77. Italics added.
3. Amanda Lenhart, Joseph Kahne, Ellen Middaugh, Alexandra Macgill, Chris Evans, Jessica Vitak, Pew Internet and American Life Project, 2007, accessed March, 2010, http://www. pewinternet.org.
4. Ibid.
5. Harmer and Smith, *The Sex Industrial Complex*, 95.
6. Belnap, *A Brain Gone Wrong*, 7–8.
7. Ibid., 8.

11

ESTABLISHING OPEN
COMMUNICATION

*The tsunami is coming. Amid this tidal wave of pornography, parents
have no choice. Let's teach our children how to swim.*[1]

TODD OLSON, LICENSED CLINICAL SOCIAL WORKER

Many dangers face our children today. One is sexual molestation.
There are genuine safety threats to them walking to school, at
the park, at a friend's, or even playing in their own front yard,
and most certainly, on the Internet. This is a sad but true fact. If
frank communication is established, a properly prepared child will
have a sense of direction when presented with pornography, bullies,
or child molesters, and a greater chance of having a fear-free, happy
childhood.

With pornography flooding the Internet, children are exposed
to it (remember, this material is sexually explicit and intended
primarily for the purpose of sexual arousal) at younger ages. Children are uneducated about its dangers and evils (not to mention
that you might not have even talked to and educated them about
sex yet).

"The kids don't have a clue. . . . They get hooked before they fully know what it is. The power of addiction is so great. It is like a magnet. If you get too close it will suck you in."[2]

START DISCUSSING HUMAN SEXUALITY

As parents or guardians of young people, one of your most essential responsibilities and one of the most important of all areas of education you need to provide to your children is about the nature of procreation and sexuality, and the essential role these will play in their lives.

Whether out of prudishness or just plain apathy, sexuality is a subject that some parents avoid openly discussing with their youth. You have to start communicating with your kids about sex. And, at the same time, you need to help them develop healthy attitudes toward sexuality. Many parents still embrace the old-fashioned value that if you talk to a child about sex, it might just make them curious. The time is now—the danger of not talking far outweighs the danger of talking.

"Provide an atmosphere where children can openly discuss these matters. Studies show that teens who come from families where sex is not discussed openly experiment with sex at an earlier age, are more likely to engage in unprotected sex, and have higher rates of teenage pregnancy when compared to teens who come from homes that have a more open climate toward issues of sex."[3]

AVERAGE AGE OF FIRST
PORNOGRAPHY EXPOSURE

"Experts say that as many as 40 percent of Americans suffer from a compulsive sexual behavior or addiction. *Furthermore, the average age of first Internet exposure to pornography is 11 years old.*"[4] This addiction could sometimes be exposure to the worst of distorted and vile sexual images at an age when some parents haven't even felt the need to discuss much of the basics of sexuality with their children yet. Obviously, for some eleven-year-olds, it's already way too late for the parent to be the one who initially communicated with them about what will become one of the most important aspects of their lives.

Since a lot of cell phones have Internet access, an eight- or nine-year-old's cell phone can have pornographic material downloaded. Or sexting can be going on—not to mention unwanted and distorted education by peers and Internet access when too young.

The topic of pornography has to be discussed with children nowadays. With young children, it can be in discussions that are mostly simple and nondescript with age-appropriate dialogue for little ones, warning them ahead of time what images they might be exposed to (situations that might arise with a friend) and how to deal with these encounters and situations. As a child reaches puberty, keep in mind that you have to expect that all boys and young men will encounter pornography, and you will need to help them be prepared and have a plan in advance with the choice already made to turn it off. They need to be armed with the knowledge of how easily it can become a compulsion and how it can damage their lives.

Remember, even though most addicts are male, don't neglect educating your girls. It's a growing problem among females, especially in chat rooms and sexting.

THE PROPERLY PREPARED CHILD

If frank communication is established, a properly prepared child can feel prepared and empowered, with some sense of control and direction when presented with pornography or predators. Additionally, it is easier to initiate discussions with them if they are displaying any of the warning signs of sexual molestation.

We want to be interactive parents. It's our privilege and responsibility to educate them about sexuality. Begin early, with age-appropriate dialogue, and continue throughout their time with you in the home. Kids won't live at home for their entire lives. They need to learn to use the Internet responsibly. It is not to be avoided or run away from. It is to be faced head on and used effectively.

Pornography thrives in dark, secret places where kids learn to lie and deceive; the best defense against the problem is openness and communication.[5]

As stated by Dorothy Maryon, a certified professional counselor, "Families should help children learn to regulate their emotions and cope with life—with its boredom, loneliness, anger, stress, fatigue and hunger. They should be busy, but also have time to relax, to meditate."[6]

Discussions of morality, developing an inner strength and spirituality, and believing in a higher power are powerful, uniting tools for families.

Dr. Jill Manning shares with us the conflicted messages about sexuality that kids get from society around them:

> The sexual maturation process begins at conception and is developed over a person's life span through the combined influence of biological phases and development, socially defined stages, and various types of relationships with others. However, children and adolescents can receive conflicted messages about sexuality from the adult society around them, and because parents often remain reluctant to discuss sexual topics with their children, today's youth are often left to their own devices to navigate the complex task of developing beliefs about sexuality and maintaining reproductive health.
>
> Studies have also shown that while there is an abundance of sexual content in the media, little is shown regarding sexual responsibility and the consequences of risky sexual behaviors, thereby complicating this developmental task further. Dolf Zillman, Dean Emeritus for Graduate Research in the College of Communication and Information Sciences at the University of Alabama, even went so far as to suggest that sexualized media is serving as "the primary agent of sexual socialization" despite findings that show young adults prefer to learn about sexuality from peers, using pornography primarily to learn about anal and oral sex . . . while adolescents prefer parents as their primary source of information.[7]

THE KEY TO SUCCESS—COMMUNICATION

"The key to success," Dr. W. Dean Belnap tells us, "still lies with that overworked word, 'communication.' Some interpret it to mean 'speak at' rather than 'speak with.' Love at home is not a 1950's sitcom outdated by today's standards," he says, "it is the cradle of positive imprinting. Togetherness, support and belonging blunt the desire to try something, 'just this once.' Families need to be led by parents. For families to make a difference, to be a reservoir of strength and purpose, they must meet these structured needs:"[8]

- Keep in contact—know the comings and goings, the friends, the pressures.

- Be together as often as possible—dinner, family night, morning prayer, evening wrap-up.

- Be genuinely concerned about the welfare of family members.

- Talk—and keep talking.

- Rally when one is floundering.

- Reach back to those who have gone before. Although society and even education have turned their backs on greatness, family histories are replete with records of men and women who struggled to rise above meager existence. The birthright of every youth is grounded in great deeds of those who had faith when life was hopeless, who fortified reason against reason, and who stood for justice, God-given purpose and vision. This is what we call heritage, and it has worth beyond date, time, and place.[9]

INOCULATE YOUR FAMILY
AGAINST THE PORN PLAGUE

Mark Kastleman, cofounder and director of education and training for Candeo, LLC., explains the "3 Simple Principles to Inoculate Your Family against the Pornography Plague:"

Our Creator knows what we are faced with in these difficult times and He has given us all the tools we need to protect ourselves and our families from this awful plague. Here are 3 simple principles you can use to protect your family.

Principle One—Teach Sacred Sexual Intimacy

The purveyors and promoters of illicit sex and pornography present their wares in a way that entices and excites the senses, appealing to the natural desires of the flesh. And like the Sirens of Greek mythology, they have deceived and lured many into their trap.

As parents, we must present the message of sacred sexual intimacy in a way that is even more powerful and attractive to our youth. We must clear away the mists of deception and teach the truth about sex. In addition, as adults, we must "walk our talk" and decide which camp we are in, which message we will allow ourselves to be attracted to and participate in. We must set the example.

How to Talk about Sacred Sexual Intimacy: If we speak about sex as "dirty," "evil" and "forbidden," we will never be able to compete with the alluring "let yourself go!" and "if it feels good do it!" messages of Hollywood and pornographers.

Instead, we must teach that Sacred Sexual Intimacy is a precious gift from our Creator. This gift is built right into our very nature as human beings. Parents have a special stewardship to teach their children how wonderful this sacred gift is. It is not something to be feared or ashamed of, but rather something to bridle and keep in reserve for the right time, place and special person—their husband or wife. Young people today need to know that sacred sexuality is worth waiting for; they need to know that it will be one of the most marvelous and fulfilling experiences of their lives.

As parents, we have a responsibility to clothe the truth as attractively as possible—to combat the glittery wrapping employed by pornographers and the sexually liberal world.

Take Care Not to Engender "Sexual Shame" in Your Children: While we should strive to teach our children to seek out entertainment that is decent and uplifting, and avoid pornography in all of its forms, we must be careful not to become "extremists" or "fanatics." Our focus should be on the beauty of human intimacy as opposed to constantly harping on the negatives.

Consider an attitude often communicated to children and

teenagers in highly religious or moral family environments: "Sex before marriage is dirty, evil, forbidden . . . and oh, by the way, be sure to save it for someone you really care about." A muddled message indeed.

When a child reaches puberty, he begins to feel sexual stirrings, arousal and attraction for the opposite sex. If he has been taught that sex is "evil" or "dirty," and/or has observed his parents acting extremely rigid or ranting about nudity, sex, pornography, etc., then this child most likely will experience sexual shame: the perception that "because sex is evil and dirty, I must be evil and dirty because I have these sexual feelings."

Yes, we should teach our children about the dangers and darkness of pornography, premarital sex, self-indulgence, etc. But of greater importance is to demonstrate appropriate love within the home, coupled with gentle teachings on the wonderful joys of intimacy. We should avoid preaching lengthy sermons, interrogating our teens after dates, ranting and raving about a questionable sitcom scene, or taking any other "extreme" approach.

Principle Two—Create and Nurture True Intimacy in Your Family Relationships

Many become vulnerable and fall prey to illicit sex and pornography because they are seeking the intimacy that is lacking in their family relationships. Illicit sex and pornography can temporarily and partially fill that void with a weak and cheap counterfeit. Afterward an even larger and deeper hole is left, one more difficult to fill with the next sexual encounter or porn-viewing session.

We Crave Intimacy: Whether we realize it or want to admit it, we crave human intimacy. We have an innate need to love and to be loved. We need to be close and connected to others, especially those in our immediate families. Brain stimulation is not enough—we need what matters to the heart.

Many of the teenagers and adults I have interviewed who got involved with Internet porn, cybersex chat rooms and/or illicit sexual encounters, reported that they were "lonely," that they felt "disconnected," that they lacked real intimacy in their lives.

You don't have to have sex to be "intimate." In fact, most human intimacy has nothing to do with sexual relations. Rather, it's about communication, understanding, appreciation, affection, mutual respect, friendship, quality time, sharing, and many more non-sexual actions and factors. One of the great preventions and protections against pornography addiction is true human intimacy, the quality and quantity of time you spend together as husband and wife, parent and child. This is what matters most.

Principle Three—Recognize When You're BLHASTed

If we're not careful, we can easily exceed our personal limits: too many balls in the air, spread too thin, we can get B.L.H.A.S.T.ed—Bored or Burned-out, Lonely, Hungry, Angry or Afraid, Stressed, Tired. (BLHASTed was first developed by my friend, therapist Dan Gray.) If we ignore these signs and continue to neglect our daily self-care, we can become increasingly weakened and vulnerable to self-medication through pornography, cybersex chat rooms and other illicit sexual activities.

And it isn't just the adults who exceed their limits. We have created an environment of "high expectation" and "super-achievement" for our children and teens as well. Please don't get me wrong—I believe we should expect a lot of our children and help them stretch, struggle and work hard to achieve worthy goals and greatness. But I believe that we sometimes push them too hard. And then our children often feel disconnected from us because of our own busy lives. Add this all together and what we often have are BLHASTed children and teens—kids who have gone beyond their limits and seek for ways to self-medicate and escape.

One of the keys to preventing porn addiction and illicit sexual behaviors is setting healthy limits, striving for balance in our lives. As adults we need to recognize our limits and help our children do the same. Pay attention to your children and recognize the signs that they are feeling BLHASTed. Don't ignore these signs! Take time for renewal, "re-creation," and healthy pleasure outlets. And pay very close attention to physical, emotional and spiritual daily self-care.[10]

10 SIGNS THAT YOUR CHILD IS BREAKING THE RULES ONLINE

Internetsafety.com provides us with some warning signs that your child may be straying into dangerous territory online.

In a perfect world, parents make the rules and kids happily follow them. But the reality is, kids are always going to test boundaries, whether on the playground or at the computer. Below are some tell-tale signs that your child may be breaking the rules for online behavior:

1. Your or your child receives unusual amounts of unsolicited email or pop-ups. This can be a sign that your child has released his personal information online. There are many enticing contests and sweepstakes, offering free MP3 players or gaming consoles, for instance, as a means of getting your child's personal information. Alert your children to the possible schemes and remind them never to give out personal information online. Take advantage of internet monitoring software to watch for further problems.

2. Your child tries to block the computer screen or quickly closes the window in which he is typing. A child's reflexes can be quick when he knows he's breaking the rules. If you notice quick or unreasonable attempts to conceal his computer screen, you should investigate further.

3. Your child spends an unusual amount of time online, especially in the evenings. Sometimes children, especially if they're home alone for extended periods, can become drawn into the social life that chat rooms and instant messaging offer. If this is the case, find out who they're talking to and what chat rooms they're visiting. While predators can be online at any hour, they are particularly active in the evenings. Internet monitoring can help you better protect your children from potential predators.

4. Your child changes her password and/or will not share it with you. It's a good idea to keep up with your child's password. If she becomes secretive about accessing her account, it may be time for you to dig deeper. Internet monitoring can alert you to such password changes.

5. Your child uses an online account other than her own. Public computers, in libraries or coffeehouses, are usually Internet ready and sometimes offer unlimited access that your child may not have at home. If your child seems to prefer the unlimited access, ask for an explanation. Internet monitoring may be needed if they won't share their reasons.

6. Your child withdraws from family or friends. Sexual predators pull children closer to them by pushing them away from family and friends. Children also tend to become withdrawn after being sexually victimized either physically or verbally.

7. You discover photos of strangers on your child's computer. Do random searches of your child's computer for files with photo file extensions such as .jpg, .tif, .gif, or .bmp. Ask your child to identify any photos of strangers, and if any are suspicious write down the information your child gives you about the person. Internet monitoring can allow you to stay a step ahead of the predators who may try to take advantage of your child.

8. Your child receives phone calls from strangers. Many predators prefer phone conversations. A predator may ask the child to call collect, and when the child calls, the predator records the phone number through caller ID. A quick phone number search using any basic search engine could also reveal your child's home address.

9. Your child receives mail, gifts, or packages from someone you don't know. Predators may try to send photos or gifts through the mail. Gifts are frequently a form of seduction used by sexual predators. If any of this activity occurs, take action immediately.

10. You discover inappropriate images or files on your child's computer. This warning sign also requires immediate action. Find out the origin of the file. If it's an image your child has voluntarily downloaded from a commercial entity, it's time to install or improve your Internet monitoring and filtering software, as well as restrict your child's Internet usage. If an individual sent the file, contact law enforcement.

Above all, trust your parental instincts. You know your child better than anyone else. Even if you cannot point to one of the signs above, when you sense something is wrong, ask questions. Use Internet monitoring software to stay abreast of your child's Internet activities. Internet usage can be eliminated completely until the issue is resolved.

Don't ever feel as if you're overreacting to the signs. If you are overreacting, those consequences are much more bearable than doing nothing at all.[11]

HOW TO REACT IF YOU FIND YOUR CHILD IS VIEWING PORNOGRAPHY

If you discover that your child is viewing pornography, it's important not to overreact or to shame them. Do not show surprise or shock. Remember, the youth is probably already feeling guilt, shame, or embarrassment about what occurred or, if older, will actually display anger that their privacy has been invaded. Denial, secrecy, lying—all are the lifeblood of pornography. Communicate and educate!

If you suspect your child has compulsive or addictive behavior with the viewing of pornography, you have to seek treatment for your child. Seeking treatment from a psychologist who specializes in sex addiction is imperative. There are many approaches to pornography and sex addiction treatment, which usually involves individual work with a psychotherapist who has skills in treating this kind of illness.

NOTES

1. Todd Olson, licensed clinical social worker, as quoted in Sara Jane Weaver, "Protecting Homes from Pornography," *LDS Church News*, The Church of Jesus Christ of Latter-day Saints, 10 Mar. 2007.
2. Sarah Jane Weaver, "The Silent Sin: Enslavement of Pornography," *LDS Church News*. 29 Nov. 2003.
3. John L. Hart and Sarah Jane Weaver, "Defending the Home Against Pornography," 21 April 2007.
4. "The Porn Stats/Ugly Statistics," The Lighted Candle Society, http://www.lightedcandlesociety.com, italics added.
5. Weaver, "Protecting Homes From Pornography." 10 March 2007.
6. Ibid.
7. Jill Manning, Testimony.

8. See Belnap, *A Brain Gone Wrong*, 122.
9. Ibid., 122–23.
10. Mark B. Kastleman. "3 Simple Principles to Inoculate Your Family against the Pornography Plague," White Papers, Candeo, http://www.candeocan .com.
11. "10 Signs Your Child Is Breaking the Rules Online," featured Internet Monitoring Article, http:// www.internetsafety.com.

12

FAMILY
SAFETY TOOLS

He that has light within his own clear breast,
may sit in the centre, and enjoy bright day:
But he, that hides a dark soul and foul thoughts,
benighted walks under the mid-day sun;
himself his own dungeon.

JOHN MILTON

The battle for the minds and souls of our children—that fight to keep our homes filled with bright days and peaceful nights (instead of allowing our children to hide a dark soul and live in "his own dungeon") is one that takes a conscious, ever-vigilant effort.

Some parents have to look back on their years of family life and child rearing burdened with sadness and grief at the realization that they didn't do it right. Many times it was not because they didn't care but simply because they didn't have knowledge pertaining to the problems facing their youth, or they didn't use the right methods of parenting or they didn't set down the right rules or show enough love and concern because they were too busy trying to make ends meet. For many parents (admittedly, sometimes through no fault of their own), it's too late and things have gone so wrong with their grown children that they now have their own grandchildren in their homes to raise.

It is, however, not too late for *you*, the parents of this young generation. Don't be afraid to communicate, to become involved, to set down rules. Don't hesitate to seek treatment for a young life you see going wrong. Use the family safety rules and tools in this chapter and review them periodically with your child. You will never regret it.

SAFEGUARDING YOUR HOME COMPUTER USE

Our children are the first generation to grow up with the Internet. Technology only changes the advantages (or disadvantages) kids and teens have. It does not change the way you parent. The rules may have changed with the Internet, but you are still the one making them. In an effort to help parents, the list below from i-SAFE America gives you tips to protect your children. Whether you are computer savvy or Internet illiterate, these tips are easy to understand, follow, and implement:

- Always keep your child's computer in an open area. Never allow a computer with Internet access in your child's bedroom.

- Communicate. There is no better tool to bridge the digital divide.

- Become a part of your child's online experience.

- Regularly review your computer files.

- Teach your child the responsible use of online resources.

- Talk to your child about online dangers. Let him know you are there to help him get out of a bad situation.

- Educate yourself on the ins and outs of the Internet.

- Talk to other parents about your experiences. It will help everyone.

- Let your child know responsible adults do not pursue relationships with minors.[1]

PARENT-CHILD INTERNET ADDICTION TEST

Dr. Kimberly Young, a psychologist and specialist on Internet addiction, developed the following test. When you add up the points, you will get a clear picture as to your child's addiction level. As stated by Dr. Young:

> The Center for Online Addiction offers hope and valuable resources to those seeking treatment for Internet addiction. Internet addiction is a type of compulsive disorder and as an organization, we are specifically dedicated to helping people who suffer from this new form of addictive behavior. How do you know if your child may be addicted to the Internet? Many parents at least ask their children how much time they're spending on the Internet. Trouble is most kids are apt to lie, especially if they're already addicted. If the computer is in their room, you have no way of knowing the truth.
>
> The following test may help you determine if you are dealing with Internet addiction in your home. It will be helpful to only consider the time your child uses the Internet for non-academic related purposes when answering."[2]

Please answer the following questions:

1. How often does your child disobey time limits you set for on-line use?

    1 = Rarely
    2 = Occasionally
    3 = Frequently
    4 = Often
    5 = Always

2. How often does your child neglect household chores to spend more time on-line?

    1 = Rarely
    2 = Occasionally
    3 = Frequently
    4 = Often
    5 = Always

3. How often does your child prefer to spend time on-line rather than with the rest of your family?

    1 = Rarely
    2 = Occasionally
    3 = Frequently
    4 = Often
    5 = Always

4. How often does your child form new relationships with fellow on-line users?

    1 = Rarely
    2 = Occasionally
    3 = Frequently
    4 = Often
    5 = Always

5. How often do you complain about the amount of time your child spends on-line?

    1 = Rarely

    2 = Occasionally

    3 = Frequently

    4 = Often

    5 = Always

6. How often do your child's grades suffer because of the amount of time he or she spends on-line?

    1 = Rarely

    2 = Occasionally

    3 = Frequently

    4 = Often

    5 = Always

7. How often does your child check his or her e-mail before doing something else?

    1 = Rarely

    2 = Occasionally

    3 = Frequently

    4 = Often

    5 = Always

8. How often does your child seem withdrawn from others since discovering the Internet?

    1 = Rarely

    2 = Occasionally

    3 = Frequently

    4 = Often

    5 = Always

9. How often does your child become defensive or secretive when asked what he or she does on-line?

    1 = Rarely

    2 = Occasionally

    3 = Frequently

    4 = Often

    5 = Always

10. How often have you caught your child sneaking on-line against your wishes?

    1 = Rarely

    2 = Occasionally

    3 = Frequently

    4 = Often

    5 = Always

11. How often does your child spend time alone in his or her room playing on the computer?

    1 = Rarely

    2 = Occasionally

    3 = Frequently

    4 = Often

    5 = Always

12. How often does your child receive strange phone calls from new "on-line" friends?

    1 = Rarely

    2 = Occasionally

    3 = Frequently

    4 = Often

    5 = Always

13. How often does your child snap, yell, or act annoyed if bothered while on-line?

    1 = Rarely

    2 = Occasionally

    3 = Frequently

    4 = Often

    5 = Always

14. How often does your child seem more tired and fatigued than he or she did before the Internet came along?

    1 = Rarely

    2 = Occasionally

    3 = Frequently

    4 = Often

    5 = Always

15. How often does your child seem preoccupied with being back on-line when off-line?

    1 = Rarely

    2 = Occasionally

    3 = Frequently

    4 = Often

    5 = Always

16. How often does your child throw tantrums with your interference about how long he or she spends on-line?

    1 = Rarely

    2 = Occasionally

    3 = Frequently

    4 = Often

    5 = Always

17. How often does your child choose to spend time on-line rather than doing once enjoyed hobbies and/or outside interests?

    1 = Rarely

    2 = Occasionally

    3 = Frequently

    4 = Often

    5 = Always

18. How often does your child become angry or belligerent when you place time limits on how much time he or she is allowed to spend on-line?

    1 = Rarely

    2 = Occasionally

    3 = Frequently

    4 = Often

    5 = Always

19. How often does your child choose to spend more time on-line than going out with friends?

    1 = Rarely

    2 = Occasionally

    3 = Frequently

    4 = Often

    5 = Always

20. How often does your child feel depressed, moody, or nervous when off-line, which seems to go away once back on-line?

    1 = Rarely

    2 = Occasionally

    3 = Frequently

    4 = Often

    5 = Always

After you've answered all the questions, add the numbers you selected for each response to obtain a final score. The higher the score, the greater the level of your child's Internet addiction. Here's a general scale to help measure the score:

• **20–49 points:** Your child is an average on-line user. He or she may surf the web a bit too long at times, but seems to have control of their usage.

• **50–79 points:** Your child seems to be experiencing occasional to frequent problems because of the Internet. You should consider the full impact of the Internet on your child's life and how this has impacted the rest of your family.

• **80–100 points:** Internet usage is causing significant problems in your child's life and most likely your family. You need to address these problems now.[3]

FAMILY INTERNET USE POLICY AND CONTRACT

Below is a sample of some Family Internet Use Policies that were adapted from CP80's website. The rules should be thoroughly discussed, signed, and put up on a wall by your computer. The breaking of these important aspects of computer use should have loss of computer privilege consequences.[4]

We agree that the Internet can be dangerous, that it is not family-friendly, and that it can only be used when we follow these rules:

1) We understand that nothing is private when we use the Internet. Anything we do on the Internet or with any device can be looked at, discussed, and reviewed for any reason and at any time. We will not keep online secrets from each other.

2) We will not change, delete, or hide any of our online activities.

3) We will only access the Internet from specific locations, times, and durations.

4) We will only access the Internet with specific devices.

5) We will ask permission before accessing the Internet from any location, at any time that, or with any device that has not been discussed.

6) We will only visit/use specific websites, games, and Internet services.

7) We will ask permission before visiting any website or using any games or Internet services that have not been discussed.

8) We will always inform our parents of any situation where the Internet could be accessed of which they are not aware.

9) We will only communicate over the Internet with the approved list of people.

10) We will ask permission before communicating with someone who has not been discussed.

11) We will ask permission before purchasing anything online, filling out any forms, or subscribing to any services or lists.

12) We will ask permission before offering personal information (name, phone numbers, email addresses, street addresses, photographs, and so on) to anyone over the Internet.

13) We will ask permission before discussing or agreeing to meet anyone from the Internet.

14) We will immediately inform our parents if anyone attempts to get personal information from us or asks to meet us in person.

15) We will avoid websites and Internet applications that allow

access to adult content (such as content that includes sexual, violent, hate-related, drug related, criminal, and similar mature content).

16) If we encounter adult content, [we will immediately turn off the monitor] and tell our parents and discuss it with them.

17) We will not download or exchange anything over the Internet without permission.

18) We will not download or exchange files that are illegal (music, movies, and so on).

19) We will not attempt to bypass any filtering software that has been installed.

20) We will not use any proxy services that hide our online activities.

Breaking any of these rules results in the immediate suspension of Internet use and the use of any device that allows us to access the Internet or view digital files.

Youth Signature(s)_____

Date: _____

NOTES

1. See "Outreach for Parents," Media Resources, i-Safe Newsroom. http://www.i-safe.org.
2. "Parent-Child Internet Addiction Test," developed by Dr. Kimberly Young, http://www.netaddiction.com.
3. Ibid. If your child has scored too high for your comfort, please refer to "A Stranger in Your Home: Keeping your Child Safe Online," http://www.netaddiction.com.

4. Adapted from "What's a Parent to Do?" Resource Categories/Family Internet Use, the CPO Foundation, Ralph Yarro, Chairman, http://www.cp80.org.

13

PORNOGRAPHY—A GLOBAL
PORNDEMIC

After reading Mark Kastleman's book *The Drug of the New Millennium*, Elly Risman, an Indonesian psychologist, educator, and champion of women's and children's rights, traveled to the United States with her colleagues in January 2009 to receive training on preventing porn addiction and protecting families.

INDONESIA'S "PORNOGRAPHY TSUNAMI"

A report written by Mark Kastleman and Dr. Randy Hyde in October 2010:

Elly Risman described the "pornography plague" that was sweeping over the land of Indonesia. Having worked in the pornography addiction prevention and recovery space for many years, we were all-too-familiar with the endless horror stories in the United States and many other parts of the world where we had been involved. But we were completely unaware of the severity or extent of the problem in Indonesia. We were very surprised to learn how rapidly pornography was overtaking their society—especially among their teens and children, even very young children. In the United States and many other countries, the pornography wave has been gaining momentum since the late 1960's and early 70's, reaching tidal wave proportions sparked by the advent of the Internet. Indonesia, seemingly, did not have this gradual build-up, but was hit later and in a much more direct manner.

It seems the massive wall of water that pounded Indonesia in 2004 was not the only "tsunami" washing over their nation! In less than a decade, pornography in Indonesia has gone from a relatively minor issue to massive proportions. How is this possible in the most populated Muslim nation on earth? How could pornography infiltrate this deeply religious society so quickly? The answer of course is "technology"—specifically, "smart phones," and other hand-held devices. It's like they were guarding the front door, while pornographers stealthily slipped in through a side window. The "older generation" of parents and grandparents were completely unprepared for the invasion of porn through hand-held technology! They naively placed these devices into the hands of millions of children and teens, with no education, limits, boundaries, or protections!

Elly's group spoke of child and teen porn addiction rates skyrocketing; children and teens committing sexual crimes against other children, and "children's jails" being filled to overflowing. They spoke of young children being encouraged to use cell phones to record themselves making their own pornography and then being paid to sell the videos online. An Indonesian government agency had just released a statistic that 65 percent of Indonesian junior high students had engaged in sexual intercourse. Many more descriptions were offered by Elly and her colleagues, too numerous and heart-breaking to mention here. And worst of all, the Indonesian government was doing nothing to put laws in place to protect children and families. They have a law against pornography, but it's not really enforced, nor can they agree on exactly what "pornography" is. In essence, in a society that is largely moral and virtuous in nature, pornography had become a "free-for-all." It is most likely, that because of their religious society, they were more naive and hence more vulnerable to the pornography scourge.

Conducting Five Days of Training in Jakarta:

Fast-forward to September 27, 2010. After nearly two years of organizing volunteers, delivering consistent print, radio and TV messages, and endlessly petitioning the Indonesian government, Elly Risman was finally granted the resources and authorization to conduct an unprecedented education and training event. Dr. Randy Hyde and Mark Kastleman were invited to conduct five days of foundational training for many of Indonesia's government officials and leading psychologists, medical doctors, educators, and religious leaders. The training centered on "pornography addiction prevention and recovery." The event was held at a conference center in Jakarta. Joining Mark and Randy was Dr. Malik Badri, one of the world's leading experts on harmonizing psychology and therapy with Islamic teachings. In his opening speech, Dr. Badri announced that this was the first conference ever held in a Muslim nation dealing with the issue of pornography!

Follow-up from Indonesia, May 2011

Following the week of training we presented in Indonesia, leading psychologists, medical doctors, educators, and religious leaders returned to their respective islands and villages to begin sharing and applying their newfound knowledge. Recent feedback indicates that it *is* making a positive difference. Unfortunately, we've also learned that child and teen use of Internet porn through cell phones is continuing to spiral out of control. The most heart-breaking result is the steep increase of Indonesian children perpetrating sexual crimes against other children—mimicking and acting out the pornography they see online.

Our Indonesian colleagues are trying to obtain funding and move three initiatives forward: 1. Translate Mark Kastleman's *The*

Drug of the New Millennium, into Indonesian and seek widespread distribution; 2. Create an Indonesian version of Candeo's online porn addiction recovery program; 3. Arrange for our return to Indonesia to conduct a follow-up and more advanced training.

AROUND THE WORLD

London (*The Observer*): Porn addicts, sex offenders, rapists, pedophiles. Increasingly, perversion is not just a problem for adults. In a basement room [of London's Portman Clinic] I met John Woods, a specialist in young people's perversions. When he trained as a psychotherapist, he began working with boys who had committed sexual offenses. . . . His patients range in age from 9 to 21, and the majority are male. . . . The clinic's most recent survey of adolescent referrals showed that sexually inappropriate behaviors dominated the caseload, with more than 50 percent of patients committing some form of sexual assault. Increasingly, Woods has found that Internet pornography is almost as serious a problem for adolescents as for adults. "I do think it has profoundly corrupting effects on youngsters, and leads them into all sorts of wrong thinking. Sex is instantly available."[1]

London (*The Mirror*): The Boy Rapists: the youngest member of this group is just 6—barely capable of tying his own shoe laces, yet somehow old enough to have committed the most serious of sexual offenses. . . . All are here for a reason most will be unable to fathom: they have raped. One of the 7-year-olds raped his 3-year-old cousin. Another forced himself on a neighbor, barely more than a baby. Another sodomized a fellow pupil in school. Shaheda Omar is a psychologist, an expert in child sex abuse. The courts turned to her when they realized the number of pre-pubescent rapists, too young to be prosecuted, was reaching terrifying proportions. "Look, this is happening," she says firmly. . . . She adds, "It is happening every day, in every part of South Africa. Boys are raping, and they are not waiting until they are 18 to start. They are getting younger and younger. What we are seeing is new," she says. We are in the middle of an epidemic . . . Children are seeing explicit sex on TV, and without parental control to explain and put it in context. A lot of children make references to pornography and this is deeply worrying. Some are obviously simply copying what they see.[2]

Australia: Mothers urge action on child-against-child sex abuse. Dianne thought she was doing the right thing when she picked up the phone to report what had happened at school to her little boy. Dianne's son had been confronted improperly by a fellow 5-year-old in a school toilet. The case has triggered impassioned debate over what is to be done about so-called sexualized intrusions on children, committed not by adults but by other youngsters. Such incidents are becoming increasingly common, according to Freda Briggs, one of the nation's top experts on child protection. Professor Briggs attributed the sexualization of children to a more highly explicit society than 10 years ago. "There's much more sex on TV. [Children are] accessing the Internet," she said. "What we are seeing is the replication of pornography, sex abuse or where they [children] have seen sex. We're paying a high price for sexual freedom; our children are being damaged."[3]

Sydney, Australia: "Net Helps Children Start Sex Attacks," *Sydney Morning Herald*, 11/26/03. Internet pornography was helping to spawn a new generation of sexual predators as young as six, child protection experts warned. . . . There had been an alarming increase in children under 10 sexually abusing other children over the past few years, most of whom had used the Internet specifically to browse porn sites, the Child At Risk Assessment Unit based at Canberra Hospital said. Cassandra Tinning, a social worker at the unit, said abusive behavior by children included oral sex and forced intercourse with other children or forced intercourse with . . . animals.[4]

Ireland: "Teenage Rape: The Hidden Story," *Irish Times*. When a children's support agency revealed this week that it had been asked to help deal with many cases of gang rape among teenagers during the past year, even rape crisis professionals were taken by surprise. . . . "We are very concerned that more and more boys are accessing their sex education from pornography," says Fiona Neary, [Rape Crisis Network of Ireland] executive director. Yet there are no programs to combat these messages from pornography, and other media, which are now very powerful. . . . Teenage Tolerance, a survey of 14- to 19-year-olds conducted by Women's Aid, found that 94% of teenage boys and 68% of teenage girls have seen pornography, mostly at friends' homes. . . . Young men in particular see pornography as a major source of information about sex, states the report. One teen interviewed confessed to having sexually abused a younger child as a direct consequence of viewing pornography, while another said that pornography had taught him how to have better sex.[5]

Ohio, USA: "Young Rape Offenders on the Rise," *Columbus Dispatch*, Ohio: An apparent jump in the number of youngsters accused of raping other children is concerning local authorities. Three boys ages 11, 12 and 14 were in juvenile court this week facing delinquency rape counts in separate cases involving children who are all younger than 10. Last year, juvenile authorities handled 33 rape cases, with 12 involving defendants between 11 and 13 years old. . . . Assistant County Prosecutor Melinda Seeds thinks easy access to pornography through the Internet and elsewhere is a factor in the number of youthful offenders. "The average age for juvenile rape offenders has been 14 or 15," she said. "I think we are going to see it get worse. What we are seeing is pornography. Some parents have it in their homes. Everybody with a computer has it available," Seeds said.[6]

New York: "School Sex Attacks Frighten Kids, Parents," *N.Y. Daily News*, 10/14/02. A kindergartner is beaten and sodomized by a gang of boys in the bathroom of his Bronx school. Two weeks later, a 12-year-old boy is jumped by 4 other boys as he crosses the playground of a Brooklyn middle school. He escapes after they try to violate him with a wooden stick. . . . Fondling is the most common assault. "You have guys walking down the hall and grabbing girls' breasts," said Dr. Elissa Brown, a child and adolescent psychologist at the NYU Child Study Center. Experts agree that most sexual abusers learn the behavior at home. Kids who commit sexual attacks often can watch anything they want on TV, have easy access to pornography, or have been repeatedly exposed to their parents' sex lives.[7]

France: "Pornography Forms French Children's Views on Sex," *Guardian* (London), 5/25/02. Concern that French children's attitude to sex is being warped by early exposure to pornography was exacerbated yesterday when eight adolescent boys were placed under formal judicial investigation for the rape of a 15-year-old classmate. Details of the alleged crime emerged the day after the publication of a survey estimating that nearly half of France's children had seen an adults-only film by the time they were 11. Most of the teenagers said they watched pornography to find out about sex, and nearly 40% said the films—almost invariably watched at home or at friends' houses while parents were out or asleep—had taught them something useful. Benoit Felix, who runs an AIDS hotline for teenagers, said it had become patently obvious that the majority of questions adolescents asked the hotline's staff were inspired by the pornography they are watching. "They want to talk about sodomy, threesomes, group sex, gang rape, bondage," he said. The language they use is that of the porn world. . . . Michela Marzano, a philosopher and psychologist, said it was becoming increasingly difficult not to relate French children's increasing exposure to pornography to the recent surge in cases of teenage collective rape. Porn does not recognize that the other person might have a different urge than yours.[8]

Taiwan: "Exposure to Internet Pornography and Taiwanese Adolescents' Sexual Attitudes and Behavior." This study examined use of Internet pornography by Taiwanese adolescents. . . . The results also indicate that Taiwanese adolescents used Internet pornography more frequently than traditional pornographic sources. Further, the exposure to Internet pornography relates to greater acceptance of sexual permissiveness and the greater likelihood of engaging in sexually permissive behavior.[9]

China: According to the Chinese Government, approximately 13% of Chinese teenagers suffer from Internet addiction and they have banned the opening of Internet cafes for the year 2007. The Government of China funded a military-style boot camp to combat the disease. Patients are males between 14 and 19 years old. This China boot camp reports a 70% recovery rate and over 1,500 youth who have received treatment at this facility operating since 2004.[10]

Amsterdam: The first Detoxification Center to treat video game addiction opened in 2006.[11]

Mumbai: The Indian Institute of Technology (IIT) adopted a measure to cut the students' use of Internet in the school dormitories after the suicide of an IIT student in October of 2005 due to Internet abuse.[12]

Canada: In *Globe and Mail*, Canadian columnist Lynn Crosbie highlights a growing concern on the Internet. History's greatest communication and networking tool is being abused. In the name of free speech it has given audience to the sordid and depraved human behaviors. "All of this grotesque fun," writes Crosbie, "does lead one to wonder how far we intend to go with our insatiable interest in the kind of images once found only on Faces of Death videos, or in hard-core porn, fetish publications and performance art." Crosbie posits that, "it may be time to rethink our artistic posturing, and concede that people are influenced by what they see, and, occasionally, like monkeys, do."[13]

Alberta, Canada: Rural teen boys are most likely to access pornography, study shows. Though being curious about sexually explicit images may seem a natural part of early adolescence, pornography is a major presence in the lives of youth, said [study author] Sonya Thompson, a masters graduate student at the University of Alberta. We don't know how we are changing sexual behaviors, attitudes, values, and beliefs by enabling this kind of exposure. Other study findings show that the majority of students [ages 13–14] surveyed, 74%, reported viewing pornography on the Internet.[14]

Germany: "German Court Tells eBay to Protect Children." The German Federal Supreme Court ruled last week that if eBay determines that a listing may be morally harmful to children, eBay must not only block the sale, but any further sales attempts. eBay must also vet those sellers in the future. The suit was brought by an association of video and entertainment media retailers, saying that eBay's offering of morally harmful media constituted anticompetitive behavior. eBay had created the serious and obvious danger by allowing a platform to distribute harmful material to children. This violates a ban on mail-order selling of harmful material. The court did indicate that if an efficient age verification system were in place, eBay would not be responsible to block harmful listings. This continues a growing trend of nations, like Israel and South Africa, taking matters into their own hands to protect their children where content providers make little or no effort. Critics of family protection measures say that the Internet and associated entities should be left to self-regulate, which essentially means no regulation and an open cesspool for our children.[15]

United Kingdom (BBC Radio): Christine Lacy, sex therapy consultant, said those with sex addiction problems felt their lives were spiraling out of control. Counselors working with teenagers have reported that the instant availability of pornographic images on the Internet and mobile phones has worrying implications for their ability to have normal sexual relationships as they grow up.[16]

NOTES

1. Available on http://www.obscenitycrimes.org.
2. Ibid.
3. Ibid.
4. Ibid.
5. Ibid.
6. Ibid.
7. Ibid.
8. Ibid.
9. Ibid.
10. Dr. Kimberly Young, "Compulsive Surfing," August 15, 2009, http://www .Netaddiction.com.
11. Ibid.
12. Ibid.
13. Ibid.
14. Ibid.
15. "German Court Tells eBay to Protect Children," http://www.cp80.org.
16. Ibid.

CONCLUSION

*If we have no peace it is because we have
forgotten that we belong to each other.*

MOTHER TERESA

What kind of society have we turned into? Aren't the majority of us decent and civilized people? Is it not the minority that hungers after the dehumanization and innocence of youth and should not the majority of us try to be the guardians of children everywhere? Shouldn't we, at the very least, let our voices be heard? As stated so well by Dr. W. Dean Belnap, "the soul of the nation, as well as individuals, has begun to teeter."[1]

The porn industry takes in billions and billions of dollars in total profit per year. One recent estimate from TopTen Reviews, an Internet research company, reported that "the industry earns $97 billion annually worldwide."[2]

That's quite a bit of income to be gained at the expense of the individual, families, and society as a whole. Let's look at the statistics:

- Americans rent upwards of 800 million porn videos and DVDs a year compared to 3.6 billion nonporn videos.

- Did you know that the pornography industry brings in more money in one year than every NBA, NFL, and MLB team combined?

- Total US revenue (2005): $12.6 billion. As of December 2005, child pornography was a $3 billion annual industry.[3]

Did you have any idea that one of our government agencies, the National Center for Missing and Exploited Children, is having such problematic job trauma related to exposure to sado-masochistic pornography that they have finally started offering and even mandating their levelheaded professional employees to seek help for job-related trauma?

The National Center for Missing and Exploited Children (NCMEC) has faced reality. It has established a "Safeguard" program to alleviate job trauma resulting from visual exposure to sado-sexual materials. NCMEC's Director of Family Advocacy Services, Marsha Gilmer-Tullis, said, "Law enforcement and the legal profession have come to understand the importance of ensuring that staff involved in this work must be taken care of emotionally and psychologically." This work refers to pornography, especially, but not only, child pornography.

"For a long time," she noted, "in law enforcement, the military, social work, and similar professions, whose job included viewing images of child pornography were afraid to admit they needed emotional help, lest this reveal an inability to perform one's job or prevent one from advancing in their career. Fortunately, that fear has been diminishing," she said. "Level-minded professionals understand that this work could create incredible psychological challenges for the viewer at present and possibly in the future."

In other words, viewing pornographic images, especially of abused children, is toxic, what is termed an "erototoxin." Such images distress even "levelheaded professionals," including FBI agents. NCMEC now has a psychologist on duty to help staff who must view this material. The April 23, 2009, addition of the NCMEC Quarterly Progress Report noted that most agencies now offer or even mandate counseling for their affected staff members rather than moving them to other jobs. In detail:

In 2007, Juliet Francis, an NCMEC psychologist, published "Helping the Helpers: Minimizing the Psychological Impact of Investigators Viewing Objectionable Material." This analysis defines "objectionable materials" as the toxic form of eros, or erototoxins. The report concluded that, although "investigators of exploited children often experience satisfaction in their work to prevent child victimization . . . viewing child pornography may increase one's risk of exposure to the effects of secondary trauma."

Exposure to pornography fits the definition of "second-ary traumatic stress disorder," given Medical News Today as "repeated and unwanted memories of the event, avoidance responses such as emotional numbness, and so-called arousal responses such as hyper-vigilance or difficulty concentrating."

Dr. Francis warns that "if denied or ignored," this trauma can so change a person's perspective that it "may impede profes-sional judgment and interfere with one's personal life."

If NCMEC staff had not experienced "emotional and psycho-logical" harm from seeing pornographic images, there would have been no justification for costly investment of time, money, and resources used to put Safeguards program in place. But inquiries NCMEC has received from other protective organizations about their own traumatized staff, demonstrates the far-reaching impact of these stimuli among professionals.

I am often asked about the children and teenagers, women, and men who are consuming "objectionable material" at home, in the office, or at school, or in prisons, hospitals, and other institutions. Do they all have a full-time psychologist available with whom they can share their, "so called arousal responses, sexual trauma, lust, fear, and shame?"[4]

This information poses an obvious question. "If the NCMEC," asks Dr. Judith Reisman, "needs to safeguard its trained adult staff from the known toxic effects of pornography, how much more vulnerable are ordinary citizens, and especially children, to these materials?[5]

The minds and the lives of our children are at stake here.

> Pornographic or erotic stories and pictures are worse than filthy or polluted food. The body has defenses to rid itself of unwholesome food. With a few fatal exceptions, bad food will only make you sick but do no permanent harm. In contrast, a person who feasts upon filthy stories or pornographic or erotic pictures and literature records them in this marvelous retrieval system we call a brain. The brain won't vomit back filth. Once recorded, it will always remain subject to recall, flashing its perverted images across your mind and drawing you away from the wholesome things in life.[6]

Take into your hearts and minds what you've read in this book and take action. Do it, if for no other reason, than for the sake of the children.

NOTES

1. Belnap, *A Brain Gone Wrong*, 7.
2. John L. Hart, "Fight to Stop Porn," The Church of Jesus Christ of Latter-day Saints, *LDS Church News*, April 14, 2007.
3. "The Porn Stats/Follow the Money," the Lighted Candle Society, available at www.lightedcandle.org.
4. Dr. Judith A. Reisman, "Picture Poison/Viewing Pornography for a Living Can Be Deadly," available on www.drjudithreisman.com.
5. See ibid.
6. Dallin H. Oaks, "Pornography," *Ensign*, May 2005.

Appendix A

RADKIDS ®

"Please don't tell me to stay safe—Teach me, or how will I know?"

WWW.RADKIDS.ORG

Other safety programs give children general guidance rules, show videos, or simply "talk" to the children. radKIDS® is dedicated to providing our children with a hands-on, activity-based, physical skill development program—empowering our children with instinctual options they need to recognize, avoid, and if necessary, respond to potential danger. When a child is approached or grabbed, the response needs to be immediate, instinctual, and absolute. Is it not time to actually teach, train, and empower our children with the skills they need to be safer in this world rather than tell them what we hope they will do when someone tries to hurt them?

Would we train our children how to swim by telling them how in the living room, then throwing them in the water?

Obviously not, so then why don't we teach and train our children how to live safer in their world today by empowering them with real skills and a positive mind-set? Teach, not tell—radKIDS® does just that.

A radKIDS® attitude, when enabled with some realistic and instinctive skills to escape violence or harm is, *"How dare you touch me!"* rather than the child who is told what to do. In danger, this child yells, *"Help me! Help me!"* Which mind-set do we want our children to have?

radKIDS® is the new and revolutionary leader in children's personal empowerment safety education and violence prevention for children. It continues to provide leadership in promoting and implementing both national as well as community-based safety education programs and services to children and parents.

With headquarters based in South Dennis, Massachusetts, radKIDS® is the national leader in children's safety. This program is brought to children and parents by the training and development of nationally certified instructors drawn from their own communities. By empowering a community with certified local instructors, the radKIDS® Personal Empowerment Safety Education package is not just a program but a true gift to the community.

The curriculum topics include:

- Home, School, and Vehicle Safety

- Out and About Safety

- Realistic Defense against Abduction

- Good-Bad-Uncomfortable Touch and More

- Stranger Tricks (including Physical Defense against Abduction)

- Self-realization of Personal Power

THE FOUR MOST PRESSING ISSUES

- Abduction

- Bullying and School Violence

- Child Abuse and Neglect

- Sexual Assault

THE HISTORY OF RADKIDS®

In the mid 1990s, a dedicated group of law enforcement professionals, self-defense experts, and concerned parents joined forces in an effort to develop a children's safety education program that would, in a fun and interactive way, combine the essential elements of risk reduction strategies with physical skill options to avoid abduction. In May 1998, after extensive research and development, the radKIDS® Personal Empowerment Safety Education Program opened its doors. radKIDS® is an innovative comprehensive safety education program for children ages preschool through twelve (kindergarten through sixth grade).

Since the organization's inception in 1998, radKIDS®, Inc. has provided the radKIDS® Personal Empowerment Safety Education Program to more than 250,000 children across North America. *As a result, statistics show that among children who have been radKID-trained, there has been a significant reduction in attempted assaults.* (Nationally, radKIDS® instructors have documented literally hundreds of disclosures and escapes from sexual assault and sexual abuse.)

In July 1999, after participating in the development and founding of radKIDS®, Stephen M. Daley assumed the responsibilities and duties of the first executive director of radKIDS®, Inc. Steve joined radKIDS® full time after an accomplished twenty year law enforcement career. At that point, radKIDS® hit the ground running. It joined the information highway in January 2000 with the establishment of www.radKIDS.org, an informational website for parents and children as well as a resource for instructors. In April 2001, radKIDS® applied for and achieved status as a not-for-profit 501(c) 3 Educational Organization. radKIDS-L, the official radKIDS list serve, was created in 2001 as an information-sharing tool for our dedicated alliance of more than 3,500 instructors located throughout the United States and Canada to exchange data or post questions.

To find radKIDS classes near you, go to their website at www.radkids.org, click on "What is radKIDS," followed by, "Find a location near you," on the drop down menu. There is nothing more important that the safety and "empowerment" of your child.

Appendix B

Filtering Software & Family
SAFETY PRODUCTS

I n this section, you will find a sampling of family protection software products and programs available on the Internet (and an
explanation on how they work). I cannot recommend or guarantee
any particular system, and I encourage you to thoroughly research
the variety of filtering software before purchasing. The information
is taken from their respective websites. Having cell phone controls,
parental controls, and filtering software on the computers in your
home, although not foolproof, are a vital part of protecting your
kids.

BSECURE.COM

- Exclusive Whole Home Filtering Option for any device
  that enters you home
  Wii
  Smartphones
  All WiFi devices

- Comprehensive Social Networking Protection
  Facebook, MySpace, Twitter & 80 others

- PredAlert Text and Email Alerts for Suspicious Activity

- Exclusive Parental Access to Child's Accounts

- Comprehensive Online Media Filter for:
  Movie MPAA ratings
  Online ESRB ratings
  iTunes filtering for explicit music

CONTENTWATCH.COM
(INCLUDES NET NANNY™)

Net Nanny™ is the only family-oriented filter that allows you to manage your home Internet use from anywhere at any time through powerful Remote Management tools. Net Nanny can be used as configured right "out of the box" or you can adjust the filter settings according to your personal preferences and needs. And monitor web browsing and instant messaging from anywhere!

COVENANTEYES.COM

Our Internet monitoring service scores websites visited for mature content and sends a report to a person you choose. Trying to monitor your family's computer in an open area isn't enough. Take control of how your family's computer is used, even when you are not at home or unable to monitor it.

- Blocks mature websites from your Windows computer(s).

- Time controls: Decide when and how long the web is used.

- Select different levels of blocking based upon age.

- Create your own list of allowed or blocked websites.

- *Download the program onto additional computers for free.*

FAMILYSAFE.COM

Family Safe provides parental control solutions for families concerned about the profanity, promiscuity, and violence in today's media and entertainment:

- TV & Video Game Time Managers (largest selection of TV & Video Game Timers).

- Filtering DVD players to control the media in your home. (A DVD player that blocks out all offensive material, has 14 different filter settings for scenes and language.)

- Next Generation of Internet Filtering is here. Filter every Internet enabled device in your house with one router. One solution covers every computer, gaming device, and iPod Touch in your home.

- The TV Guardian filters profanity from your videos, TV, DVD, Satellite, and Cable, While You Watch!

- CarChip Pro—Black Box for Your Car. Website contains many other innovative products for family safety.

INTERNETSAFETY.COM

- Used as a rehabilitation resource by the top pornography addiction recovery ministries

- Two-time winner of PC Magazine's Editors Choice

- Award Rated #1 by Consumer Reports

- Safe Eyes has been a lead innovator (first to filter YouTube, first filtered browser for the iPhone, filter online TV).

Whether at home, on the go, or at your business, school or church, Safe Eyes puts you in control of your Internet. With thirty-five categories of blocking, as well as keyword blocking and blacklists, InternetSafety.com solutions can easily be tailored to your values. All solutions are easy to install and use, and all give you peace of mind knowing that your family, employees, students, or congregation is protected from harmful online content.

MYMOBILEWATCHDOG.COM

My Mobile Watchdog safeguards your child while using cell phones and immediately alerts you if he or she receives unapproved email, text messages, or phone calls.

MMWD was originally called RADAR and was provided to law enforcement on an as-needed basis. It quickly became apparent how big the problem of child exploitation was and how a new generation of exploiters were using mobile phones to gain unprecedented access to children.

To date, law enforcement has used My Mobile Watchdog to arrest and convict over 300 child predators. 90% of those convicted did not have a prior record and were not registered sex offenders.

SPECTORSOFT.COM

SpectorSoft provides award-winning software products that empower parents to monitor the online activity of their children and identify conduct and pornographic content that may jeopardize their safety and well-being. Spector Pro and eBlaster record every detail of what a child does on a computer—all chats, instant messages, emails, the websites they visit, what they search for, what they do on MySpace and Facebook, the pictures they post and look at, the keystrokes they type, the programs they run, and much more. Spector Pro also provides a video-like playback feature so parents can see exactly what was on a child's screen, and includes tabs for popular social networking sites such as MySpace and Facebook.

eBlaster is a remote surveillance product that captures all PC and Internet activity and sends an easy-to-read Activity Report to any email address you choose, as often as you like. Both products are available in Windows and Mac versions and can be installed on a home computer, laptop, or Netbook in less than five minutes.

YOUDILIGENCE.COM

- Protect your children on Facebook, MySpace & Twitter

- Stop cyber-bullies & web predators from hurting your child

- Monitor social network activity when they use any computer or mobile phone

- Customize specific key words you want to track

- Receive real-time detailed email alerts

- Access their online "friends" public profile information.

- It doesn't matter if a kid uses a PDA, a cell phone, his aunt's computer, or is on a class trip to China—YouDiligence is going to grab it as soon as it's posted.

Appendix C

Movie GUIDES

RATING MOVIES

This book wouldn't be complete without including information on movie rating websites. These are only an example of what is out there. I do not recommend any one program or product. I do warn you to thoroughly explore all protection options and remember to keep updating whatever systems or programs you choose.

KIDS-IN-MIND.COM

We enable adults to determine whether a movie is appropriate for them or their children, according to their own criteria. Unlike the MPAA we do not assign an inscrutable rating based on age but three objective ratings for sex/nudity, violence/gore & profanity, on a scale of 0 to 10, and we explain in detail why a film rates high or low in a specific category; we also include instances of substance use, a thorough list of discussion topics that may elicit questions from children, and the message the film conveys. Since our system is based on objective standards, not the viewer's age or the artistic merits of a film, we enable adults to determine whether a movie is appropriate for their own children.

COMMONSENSE.ORG

Common Sense Media is the leading independent, non-profit organization dedicated to improving the lives of kids and families by providing the trustworthy information, education, and independent voice they need to thrive in a world of media and technology. They are the nation's most used and trusted source for age-appropriate ratings and information on movies, apps, television, books, music, websites, and video games. They feature more than 14,000 media reviews, all based on child development guidelines.

Common Sense Media also provides parents with advice on how to deal with today's challenges of cyberbullying, texting, and sexting, as well as how to deal with age inappropriate content and computer addiction. Parent tips, videos, and tech tips, and reviews are available on our website (www.commonsense.org); used in schools in all 50 states; and they are viewed by more than 10 million people a year through partnerships with leading media, technology, and entertainment companies. For more information, visit www. commonsense.org

INDEX

G

H

I

J

K

ABOUT THE
AUTHOR

Mary was born and raised in California. Her most challenging and matchless role in life was raising seven children. She worked for the Air Force, the Department of Defense, and as a nurse in private practices for many years. She is the published author of two other books—*Angels in Our Midst* and *The Holy Ghost, the Third Member of the Godhead*. Mary resides in Lehi, Utah, with her best friend and eternal companion, Martin.